CU00841311

The A to Z
of Spanish Culture

Beyond toros and flamenco

Pilar Orti
with additional material by Paul Read

If you enjoy the autobiographical aspects of this book, check out Pilar Orti's memoir: *"Hi, I'm Here for a Recording. The ordinary life of a voiceover artist."*

Contents

Introduction to the Third Edition

When I first wrote 'The A to Z of Spanish Culture', I was hoping to sell a few books and make enough money to cover the costs of book formatting and cover design. So I was very pleased with how well the book was received by those with an interest in Spain and to my surprise, my little book about my country of origin made the recommended reading lists of academic programmes in both schools and universities.

An A-level Spanish teacher called Cristina told me that she recommends the book to the students in her London school precisely because it is such a condensed read. "Once they've read the book, they can identify which aspects of Spanish history and culture interests them most, and they can go and study those topics in depth."

When I first found out how the book was being used, I considered updating it but felt too removed from the country to be able to do so. I'd also stopped publishing the "*Spain Uncovered*" podcast, so I had little motivation to catch up with and share what had gone on in Spain. But when last year a generous reviewer pointed out that "An update to 2017 would be great as a lot has happened there," I thought, "Right, now is the time to do this."

I'd written 'The A to Z' to show how much Spanish society had evolved during the 1980s, 90s and first decade of the 21st Century. I thought the country had evolved and changed massively during that time. What I didn't expect was there would still be more twists and turns on their way.

Introducing Paul Read

In the first edition of 'The A to Z', I said everything I had to say about Spain. I've now been away from the country for more than 25 years and I don't stay much up to date with what's going on there. This means I'm not the best person to update this book, so I reached out to the only other writer who I knew would enjoy putting down some brief words about those aspects of Spanish society and politics that had undergone the most significant changes since the last edition of the book.

Luckily, in between his own projects (which mainly involve teaching TaiChi online), Paul Read aka "Gazpacho Monk" accepted to take on the task of writing a few paragraphs to bring this 'A to Z' up to date. So, what's new then?

- There is a new, *M is for Más Movidas* chapter which summarises the recent change in Spain's political landscape, as well as the rising number of corruption cases. Paul has done a brilliant job of explaining some very complex court cases, some of which are still ongoing (which means we had to tread carefully when laying them out in front of you).

- Speaking of corruption, I've expanded the chapter on *C is for Corona* to include the recent scandal involving members of the Spanish Royal Family using some of Paul's notes.

- The chapter **Ñ is for Ñ** has been expanded to include the current situation in Cataluña. In the original chapter, I didn't go into the different nationalist movements in much depth. That was because I have never had much of an identity as a Spaniard, and so I've never empathised with those holding strong nationalistic views. Even though I've been aware of the quest for independence from both Basque and Catalans all my life, I never took much interest. However, at this point in time, to have a book about Spanish culture that didn't cover the Catalan movement in some depth would be to miss out a very important moment in contemporary history.

- In the new section **When Ñ Becomes NY,** I have left Paul's words almost intact. He's always had an interest in the history of Cataluña (which is at the centre of his book *"Forgotten Stories From Spain: 1984 and The Spanish Civil War"*) and once again, he's been able to summarise clearly a very complex situation. Unfortunately, this chapter has an open ending, reflecting the unresolved status of this episode in history.

Paul has also provided me with bits and pieces to bring other chapters of the book up to date. I've peppered them around and adapted them to my own voice as much as possible.

Finally, in the interest of balancing his own opinions with facts (or at least with other opinions in the public arena), Paul has provided us with the long list of sources he used while writing the new pieces. You can find them all in the appendix Vocabulary and References.

I hope you enjoy this new edition, which, as well as facts and my own stories, now also includes someone else's voice. Let's now travel just a little bit back in time as I tell you how the idea for this little book began…

Pilar Orti
London, March 2018

Introduction

When I told my uncle I was going to write the A to Z of Spanish Culture he replied:

"Pero eso... va a ser mucho trabajo."

("But that is going to be a lot of work.")

Or something along those lines.

I then explained that I wasn't going to write anything akin to an encyclopedia – each letter would not have numerous entries but would provide the heading for each chapter. The chosen word would open up a whole aspect of Spanish culture. "Culture" in its broadest sense: food, history, art, traditions...but more than anything, a way of living. Each chapter would be short, informative, entertaining and even useful for those visiting Spain.

It's taken me over a year to put this short book together, a "light-hearted look at Spanish culture" as someone on the web put it. During that time, Spain has been plunged into a dark hole of unemployment, corruption, large debt and even social unrest. The country is facing challenges now it never thought it would, certainly none that I ever had to face when I was growing up in the 80s. I have continuously returned to the different chapters as events have unfolded in Spain, in the hope of reflecting the present as much as the past.

Having lived in London for over 20 years, I have heard so many myths and assumptions about life in Spain that I hope I can put some right. The most frequent assumption being that it's always warm and sunny in Spain. Well, Spain is quite large and although Andalucía, Levante and the Canary Islands enjoy pretty decent weather all year round, the North experiences its good share of rain while in Madrid, temperatures can drop to minus 5 degrees Celsius in the winter.

The content of this book jumps from one aspect of Spanish culture or life to another, so reading it might be a bit like landing in the middle of Spain and being exposed to a number of experiences. It intends to be part memoir, part history lesson and part magnifying glass to Spanish society today.

This book also comes with a warning: some chapters might be lightly sprinkled with a wave of nostalgia, from someone who grew up in Madrid in the 80s. As a result, some content might be a bit "retro" and I know I have missed aspects of life outside the capital. 'The A to Z of Spanish Culture' presents a condensed version of Spain: mainly through the eyes of an ex-pat (as in Spaniard who set up shop in London), who has often struggled with how much or how little she carries of Spain inside her.

I have tried to fill in any gaps in my own experience with research and by asking people more clued up than myself; this means I have discovered things I never knew such as the fact that my saint's day, which is on the 12th October, is not celebrated on the day when "my Saint" appeared on top of a pillar; or that the most famous lines of the play 'Fuenteovejuna' do not appear in the play exactly as they are often quoted.

By chance I ended up making a living in London as a Spaniard: working as a Spanish voiceover has meant that I've kept up to date with culture and language (kind of: what's the current version of *guay*?) and my frequent trips to Spain have allowed me to experience the change in society over the past twenty years first hand. So I suppose this book could have also been called '*Pilar's A to Z of Spanish Culture*', as it has as much of me in it as it has of Spain.

The chapters of this book are short and I have included a small vocabulary list at the back for reference, in case you want to learn a bit of Spanish. You can also read some of the original contributions from my friends and family in 'From the Horses' Mouths'.

And if you want to hear more about Spain and the origin of some Spanish proverbs, there are about 30 episodes of the 'Spain Uncovered' podcast still available for you to listen to, with guest interviews and solo shows.

For now,

¡Qué aproveche!

Pilar Orti

London, June 2012

A is for Amor

Love.

Any contact with a group of typical Spanish people will show you their love of many things. Love of their cars; love of their food; love of football; love of their holidays; love of everyday life; love of trashy television...

Many of these all come together in the way the Spanish love to be with other people.

Restaurants, *cafeterías*, bars, it doesn't matter if they are completely packed, they'll still get more people through the door, especially if there is a football match and the television is on. Young people will go out in *pandillas*, (gangs, but without the violent connotation) which over time will evolve into more civilised, adult groups. It will, however, still be common for these groups to go out for dinner together, go out for drinks together and even travel abroad together. The Spanish love being in packs.

Holiday destinations are overcrowded during the public holidays, especially in the summer when everyone seems to take their holidays at the same time. In fact, some businesses and companies request that their employees take their holidays in August. I know it's not a phenomenon exclusive to Spain but this results not only in overcrowded beaches and towns, but also in long, long traffic jams.

If you decide to leave the city at the same time as everyone else to make the absolute most of your holiday, you will get stuck for hours in a traffic jam (*atasco*) or travel *en caravana* at danger-ously high speeds. Travelling *en caravana* often means driving dangerously fast and dangerously close to other cars. If at any moment anyone has to break, it will lead to accidents *en cadena* (a rear-ending chain), especially in bad weather. I've been a pas-senger in cars driving in the heavy rain *en caravana* at 120 km per hour - scary stuff.

As a result, the beginning and end of every holiday period (*operación salida* (operation: exit) and *operación retorno* (oper-ation: return)) tend to be marked by images of smashed cars on T.V. and the latest number of fatalities on the road. The only silver lining to this very dark cloud is that as a result, the number of organs available for transplant is quite high. In Spain, you need to opt OUT of the transplant register if you don't want to donate your organs when you die, which results in healthy organs being available for transplant after these horrific car crashes.

In 2010, 1,730 people died on the road, but luckily, this number is falling every year as the roads and cars get better and as drivers become more civilised. The road system has improved much in Spain over the last 30 years as a result of significant European Union funding, even to the point that it is rare not to find road works on your way when you travel. A journey by car from Madrid to Valencia used to take about 7 hours and can now be done in 3.5. The cars you see on the road are quite decent too.

The Spanish love travelling by car. They use the car to go everywhere. To travel into the city, to get through the city, to get out of the city. A shame, because public transport tends to work rather well. The tube system in Madrid, for example, is fantastic –

it's clean, it runs on time and the carriages have air conditioning in the summer. The train system can be quite impressive too. The seats are comfortable and the network enjoys some high-speed lines. Though not affordable to everyone, the high-speed train (AVE, *Alta Velocidad Española*) and those that use its tracks can save you a lot of time.

Traffic in Spanish cities is as bad as in most European countries. Each city copes as best as it can, sometimes by adopting social norms which make everyone's lives easier. For example, in Valencia (which by the way also has a decent public transport system), parking spaces are scarce. As a result, it is very common to find cars double-parked and sometimes, triple-parked. The *valencianos* have come up with a way of this being acceptable: feel free to double park, but don't leave your handbrake on. In this way, if another car wants to leave and you are blocking their way, the driver can just push your car a bit until he/she has enough room to get out. Not bad.

Amor por la comida

The Spaniard's love of food is obvious if you consider how popular *tapas* are outside Spain. Spain has exported not just a couple of dishes but also a whole range of them. (I will talk about some of the most popular *tapas* in *T is for Tapas.*) The Spanish, in general, have quite a strict eating timetable. You might be able to be served in a restaurant from 1.30- 3.30 pm. *Cafeterías* and bars are likely to serve you food all day; but don't try to have dinner in a restaurant before 8.30pm. I still remember when my parents and I went out for their anniversary dinner about ten years ago. We've always eaten early by Spain's standards and we arrived at 8.30pm to be greeted by a complimentary glass of *cava* as the kitchen hadn't opened yet. Love of food, love of wine, love of good service.

Every time I go out to a restaurant in Spain, I'm still struck by the pride and skill of the professional waiters. Far from being a job used to earn some pocket money in the summer or to fill in the time while waiting for a dream job, waitressing has always been a respectable profession in Spain, where the *camareros* and *camareras* understand their essential role in the ingrained Spanish tradition of regularly eating out. I just hope this tradition doesn't die out as more chains open in the high street.

Another aspect of eating out that might surprise visitors to Spain is that the Spanish don't tip much. This is probably because having breakfast at a *cafetería* or having lunch in a restaurant is part of every day life and therefore tipping regularly would be expensive. Compare this to other countries where sitting down at a café or eating out with your family is more an exception than the rule, and you will understand why the Spanish tend to tip so little.

Amor por los amigos

"Quien tiene un amigo, tiene un tesoro."
(Whoever has a friend, also has a treasure.)
I've already mentioned the popularity of the *pandillas*, those groups of friends (*amigos*) that hang out together. While the

Spanish are not famous for organising themselves to pursue a common interest or take on a business opportunity, they are very creative when it comes to getting together to have a good time.

For this reason, the traditional *peñas* are still alive and kicking. You can think of the *peñas* as formal *pandillas*, groups which needed a formal structure under the dictatorship, in order to allow young people to come together without the risk of being dispersed by the authorities. Nowadays, they come into all their glory during the local *fiestas*, parading through the streets, usually with their music band leading the way.

Amor por el amor

Public displays of affection are common in Spain. You might see friends holding hands, parents affectionately holding their children and couples kissing and embracing in the middle of the street. The concept of "personal space" does not really exist amongst your typical Spaniard; if it does, it disappears when you first meet someone and kiss them on each cheek. Two kisses is the standard greeting in Spain between two women or a woman and a man; in the newer generations, men might also give each other two kisses or a hug, but if they haven't met before, a more formal handshake is the norm.

The most popular set of love poems are those written by Gustavo Adolfo Béquer, poet and writer who lived during the 19th century. His *Rimas* have become part of Spanish popular culture, pretty much like the poems of García Lorca (more about him in **D is for Duende**). I remember as a teenager I had a folder with separators (many years before *Apple* meant anything else but a fruit) where my friends would write, scribble and leave notes for me. One of such bits of poetry came from Béquer and it condenses the ephemeral nature of love better than anything else I have ever read.

Los suspiros son aire y van al aire.
Las lágrimas son agua y van al mar.
Dime, mujer, cuando el amor se olvida
¿Sabes tú adónde va?

Sighs are but air exhaled into air.
Tears are but water running towards the sea.
Do you know, woman, when love is forgotten,
Do you know where it might go?

B is for Botellón

A way of drinking that has become extremely popular in the 21st century (although it's by no means an innovative way of partying) is the *botellón*.

Botella means bottle and *botellón* is the modern term given to the gathering of young people in an open space, sharing bottles of alcoholic drinks. Sometimes the youngsters just sit around a bench in a park; other times they might congregate around the boot of a car, where they have their improvised mini-bar. The more sophisticated University students used to purchase everything they needed from the local stores. A *botellón* pack would include tube glasses, a bottle of alcohol, ice, two-litre bottles of soft drinks and snacks. The students would create their own open-air bar with these contents and then clear up after themselves before moving on at 2am to the bars.

This fashion began to threaten the peaceful life of the *barrios* (neighbourhoods) and in 2002, the government tried to put an end to this by trying to introduce a law referred to as the "*Ley Antibotellón*", which would have put an end to groups of people drinking alcohol in the street. While the law was not finally passed by the central government (you can imagine how unpopular they would have become), many regions began to legislate against this kind of activity.

Sharing drinks in this way precedes the 21st century of course, but the economic situation has driven a lot of drinking out of the bars and into the open spaces. The *litrona* (a 1-litre beer bottle) has always been the shared drink of choice, while in the 80s the *minis* became the fashionable way of sharing your drink (and your spit). A group of friends would order a *mini de cerveza* (one litre of the drink, also known as *cachis* in Bilbao) and share it between them. The more sophisticated ones (or, some would argue, those with least respect for the art of drinking) would order other kinds of drinks in litre form, such as vodka and orange or *leche de pantera* (panther's milk), a cocktail made of rum, milk and cinnamon. No party games would surround the drinking from these large containers, just conversation and maybe one extra cold or too...

Drinking alcohol is part of everyday life in Spain, though one would like to think it happens in moderation: a glass of wine with dinner or a *caña* with your *aperitivo* and maybe quite a few *copas* (drinks with spirits) when you go out with your friends late at night. Children might taste alcohol with their food at special occasions, such as *vino con gaseosa* (wine with soda) which is a popular drink during family celebrations. (For more, see **V is for Vino**.)

During the festive seasons, alcohol consumption increases dramatically. As in most Western countries, Christmas is the season to be jolly and excessive, so the alcohol intake increases as people fill their bellies with food and drink.

As well as drinking wine with your food, you can also have a *carajillo*, coffee with brandy. If you just feel like putting a sweet end to your meal, make sure you enjoy the often complementary *chupitos* (shots of spirits) or how about trying the very Spanish *pacharán* – an anisette-based drink which can be drunk straight or on the rocks.

Rumour has it that the *controles de alcoholemia* increase during the Christmas period and you are likely to see police cars around every corner, waiting patiently for a car to exceed the speed limit or exhibit some strange locomotion. With the introduction of the "points system" in 2006 whereby drivers lose some of their allocated 12 points when they break the law, it seems like less people are driving after drinking alcohol. The threat of losing up to 6 points, thus being half way to losing your driving licence for at least six months, has proved to be a much more efficient way of reducing drink-driving than Stevie Wonder's campaign "*Si bebes, no conduzcas*" (If you drink, don't drive).

In the 80s, the artist Stevie Wonder headed the campaign "*Si bebes, no conduscas*". (It should be "*conduZcas*", but Stevie turned the 'z' into an 's'.) I'm not sure it made a difference. Since then, the government's driving campaigns have got more and more hard-hitting, to the point that they are sometimes unbearable to watch.

As I mentioned earlier, the main problem with the *botellón* is that it threatens the peace of the traditional *barrios*. Though these are being replaced by more impersonal versions, there are still places in Spain where you can find all the elements of a typical neighbourhood.

El barrio

A typical *barrio* will be formed of blocks of flats, neatly clumped together surrounding a play area where children can play safely in their *pandillas*. It's quite common to hear a voice calling out around dinner-time:

"¡Manolo! ¡A cenar!"

Calling for Manolo (wherever he is hiding or playing ball) to come back home for dinner. It's also common to hear a child's voice calling: "¡*Mamá*!" in the hope that their mother will hear them from the fifth floor and come out onto the balcony to see what they want.

Key to the neighbours' wellbeing, is the presence of the *portero* or *conserje*, the concierge. Mainly present in the middle-class and well-off neighbourhoods, the *portero* is key to the families' health. The *porteros* (or *porteras* if they are women) are there during working hours to pick up deliveries; they're there to keep the communal parts tidy; they can liaise between the maintenance men or workmen or builders and the neighbours; and they can let you know what's going on in the neighbourhood or your block of flats. Who's having their bathroom redecorated, who's having a problem with the heating... a good *portero* knows what's going on.

In a typical barrio, you will find a *quiosco*, a freestanding newsagents where you can buy your magazines and daily press, along with *chucherías* (sweets and other deliciously addictive foods) like *chicles* (chewing gum) and *gusanitos* (corn puffs). There used to be a time when you could also buy tobacco and cigarettes from them, but this trade is now restricted to the *estancos*, where you can also buy stamps.

A *barrio* might also have a *mercería*, (haberdashery) where you can buy anything and everything needed in a woman's wardrobe from tights, through to elastic, thread, all kinds of buttons...

Next to the *mercería*, you might also find a *ferretería*, with everything you'll need for the home: screws, tools, taps, etc.

Almost every household will buy every day *una barra de pan* (a stick of French bread). This can be bought at the *panadería*, where you will probably also be tempted by *cuernos* (huge pastries covered in chocolate with liquid chocolate inside), croissants and *donuts*.

Ah... (a nostalgic sound), the *donuts*. They form part of every child's life and even of popular culture. *"¡Ahí va, los donuts! ¡Ahí va, la cartera!"* was a very famous slogan from a 1980s publicity campaign promoting "Donuts" a brand of big doughnuts. A boy of about 10 years old was so careful not to forget to take his donuts to school that he ended up leaving behind his schoolbag (*cartera*) at home. *"¡Ahí va!"* is a common Spanish exclamation, usually following a realisation. It is still common to hear people echoing this advert when they watch someone realising they have left something behind.

Bars of chocolate, snacks and all different kinds of *chucherías* can also be found at the *panaderías*. If you are really lucky, your *panadería* might also have a *pastelería* (*pastel* means cake), or you might find that as a separate store. The Spanish don't consume much chocolate, but they really like their *pastelitos*, which are small *pasteles*, or cakes. *Pastelitos* are bought by weight and they are usually eaten on special occasions.

Most neighbourhoods will also have a *frutería, verdulería, carnicería* or *pescadería* (fruit store, grocery store, butchers, fishmonger's) and they might all be found in the *mercado* (market). However, all this is gradually disappearing as the Spanish, like most of Western Europe, have really taken to the supermarkets and their smaller franchises. For example, Mercadona, the super-market chain of Valencian origin, is doing particularly well – even being mentioned in the Harvard Business Review February 2012 issue as one of four companies featured in an article about creating excellent conditions in the workplace.

Over the past ten years, Chinese immigration has given rise to a new type of shop, those commonly known as *los chinos* (the Chinese), which are stores where you can find almost anything you are looking for at a very cheap price. These stores are usually open longer hours than other shops and have become the local convenience stores. The Chinese have established themselves as successful storekeepers and are now branching out into other types of businesses, like nail salons.

Friendships and feuds will emerge in the barrios. Young children will play together for hours on end; teenagers will hang around in their *pandillas* and will begin to go out (*salir*), espe-cially in the summer when the warm nights allow them to hang around outdoors into the early hours of the morning. Young par-ents might drop their kids off with a neighbour to have a night out and adults might enjoy going out for cups of coffee or a drink and play cards by the swimming pool on Sunday afternoon (in the summer, of course).

Most flats will be managed by a *mancomunidad* (a manag-ing agent) and each block of flats will have a rotating president and vice-president, who will call and chair regular *reuniones de vecinos* (residents' meetings or literally, meetings of neighbours). A structured way of keeping everyone involved and informed about issues that might arise in the building – you can also see how feuds can easily develop.

Barrios differ from one part of the city to another and from city to city. While they can be safe places to grow up in and areas where everyone feels part of a community, they can also be areas of deprivation and hubs of crime. (Not that any of this is particular to Spain, of course.) For an accurate portrayal of one of Madrid's neighbourhoods in the 1990s, you can watch the film '*Barrio*' by Fernando Leon de Aranoa. It's a little bit tough but also quite charming. Just like life itself.

C is for Corona

La corona, the Crown.

Far from wanting to turn this chapter into a history lesson, I think it's important to know a little bit about the events that took place in the twentieth century to understand the image the Spanish have of the Royal Family today.

One Republic, Two Dictators and Three (well, two and one who never got the crown) Kings.

In 1923, Miguel Primo de Rivera headed a coup that led him to become the head of the Spanish state for seven years. The monarch at the time, King Alfonso XIII, supported him fully, a fact I ask you to hang onto - its significance will become apparent later. When Primo de Rivera stood down as dictator and left for France, Spain's Second Republic was established.

In 1936, Francisco Franco led a military coup which kicked off a civil war dividing the country in two: the right and the left. (Up to this day, most Spaniards still think that there are only two ways of viewing the world: from the left or from the right, although in a survey by the *CIS* in 2011, about 32% of them considered their political views to be somewhere in the middle.) The Civil War lasted three years and resulted in a military dictatorship that ended in 1975. During this time, Franco refused to let the new heir to the throne, Don Juan de Borbón, anywhere near the Spanish crown. Instead, in 1969, he passed a law that gave monarchic powers to Don Juan's son: Juan Carlos I.

Freedom

In 1975, Franco died. (For more on the civil war and Franco, see the next chapter, **D is for Duende.**) For quite a few months, the Spanish population waited to see whether they would continue to be ruled by a dictator or whether democracy might finally arrive. The King kept Arias Navarro at the head of the civil government, as he had been in charge over the last years of the dictatorship as Franco's health deteriorated. In 1976, Juan Carlos took the first steps in changing the way Spain was ruled by asking a young politician, Adolfo Suárez from the party UCD (*Unión Centro Democrático*, Democratic Centre Union) to become the country's president.

With freedom of speech came also the freedom to choose your own religion, as well as the right to choose your country's government. In 1977, Suárez was elected president and even made the cover of the USA's TIME magazine, with the headline "Democracy Wins". A year later, a constitution was drafted and approved by the Spanish people on the 6th December, a date which has been a national holiday ever since.

History (almost) Repeats Itself

A few years later though, Suárez felt like he was losing the support of the Spanish population and his party and he resigned.

On the 23rd February 1981, Leopoldo Calvo Sotelo was ready to become the second president of Spain's new democracy. All Spanish eyes (or most of them) were glued to the television to witness another event with democracy at its core.

And then it happened.

Under the counting of the votes, a commotion.

A bit of noise outside.

The President of the Congress asking softly, "¿*Qué pasa?*" ("What's going on?")

And then a lieutenant, in full *guardia civil* gear, wearing the classic *tricornio* (a three-pointed hat worn by the civil guard) entered the Congress, with a gun in his hand.

"*Quieto todo el mundo.*" ("Everyone, stand still.")

Followed by:

"Al suelo, al suelo todo el mundo." ("Everyone, down on the floor.")

Then more military, this time with machine guns. A few shots and most of the politicians were forced to crouch down in their seats. Most except Suárez and Gutierrez Mellado, a military man who was Minister of Defence at the time and who directly challenged the intruders. Luckily for him, he was just pushed around a bit and not shot. I was watching this on television and I remember Suárez shouting at the military, "I'm the president, I'm the president," as if thinking that his resignation had caused the mess and wanted to take it back.

Looking for footage of the event on YouTube, I found a

video with commentary from a radio journalist. You don't need to speak Spanish to hear the panic in his voice as he realised what was happening. Meanwhile, the camera darts everywhere following the bullets from the machine guns and finally it stops, pointing at the ceiling. A male voice is then heard saying:

"No intentes apuntar la cámara que te mato."
("Don't try to point the camera or I'll kill you.")

You can imagine every Spanish heart sinking very low as they watched this coup. People who'd fought for freedom of speech; politicians who had been involved in the transition to democracy (*la Transición*), young people like me (I was 9 years old) who knew they had narrowly escaped repression and oppression and could see clearly in their parents' faces the words "No, please, not again..." Everyone stared at the TV, waiting to see if this event would affect their lives.

The phone rang in my house. It was the Danish mother of a friend of mine, calling to ask for advice. What was going on? What should she do? Send the kids to school the following day? Keep them home?

Luckily, all this happened at a time when TV was already a part of most Spanish households. Calvo Sotelo (who was being elected president on the 23rd February) points out in his book *Memoria viva de la transición*, that watching the drama unfold on T.V. stripped the coup of any mystery and therefore, of some of its impact. There wouldn't be time for rumours or urban myths to emerge, as everyone had had the chance to witness the event live on T.V. Just as the Spanish population saw the event live, they also witnessed how it was knocked on the head by a simple, straightforward speech.

The Royal Family - from Heroes to Villains

Remember I asked you to hold on to the fact that king Alfonso XIII fully supported the military rebellion during his reign? Here is why.

On the evening of the 23rd February 1981, young Juan Carlos I sat in front of the cameras and asked the Spanish people to defend the constitution and Spanish democracy. Antonio Tejero Molina, his moustache and all the other *guardia civiles* had no support from the king, also head of the armed forces. The army entered the congress and put an end to the coup. Juan Carlos won a special place in most Spanish hearts, having acted in a much more democratic way than his grandfather and giving the rebels no choice but to surrender.

As far as I remember, the Spanish Royal Family were always welcome by the Spanish as the country's ambassadors, except for the Republicans of course. The high-ranking civil servants are invited to a public event celebrated on the King's birthday, the 5th January (how apt, on the day of the arrival of the "three kings" - see *U is for Uvas*), maybe as a way to stay in touch with the people. The Greek Queen Sofia, always at his side, has always appeared stern, elegant and correct while their three children, Cristina, Elena and Felipe stayed out of the spotlight for quite a long while.

In the last few years though, the members of the Royal Family have hit the headlines more and more often, for various reasons. The then Prince, *príncipe Felipe*, the heir to the throne, married the journalist Letizia Ortiz Rocasolano, raising a few eyebrows and providing the real-life event on which the T.V. mini-series '*Felipe y Letizia*' is based.

King Juan Carlos himself grabbed the spotlight when he had a go at Hugo Chávez at a meeting, when the Venezuelan head of State kept interrupting Spain's president at the time, Rodriguez Zapatero. In what became a very famous sound bite, Juan Carlos just plainly said to Chávez:

"*¿Por qué no te callas?*" ("Why don't you shut up?")

Another video worth watching on YouTube.

While Felipe's marriage to a non-Royal and Juan Carlos' outburst were great gossip fodder, a more serious event took place in April 2012. In the middle of an economic crisis that saw many lose their jobs and being evicted from their homes, the King broke his hip... while shooting elephants in Botswana.

Twitter went completely mad, with people complaining about the fact that while Spain was in crisis, the King was out hunting elephants. I loved this very creative tweet from @ XoseMorais:

Efecto mariposa: yo pago mis impuestos en España y un elefante muere en Botsuana.

(The Butterfly Effect: I pay my taxes in Spain and an elephant dies in Botswana.)

What made this even worse, was that King Juan Carlos was at the time honorary president of the World Wildlife Fund. The King, who was 74 years old, apologised to the cameras as soon as he was able to walk out of the hospital: a sincere apology with a promise of "never again", a rare occasion seen in Spanish public and political life. Just a shame that the King who saved Spain from another dark era managed to screw things up so near the end of his reign.

Spanish Monarchy 2.0

King Juan Carlos abdicated on 17 June 2014, pushing his eldest son Felipe on to the throne. Spaniards felt that perhaps it was time to show their feelings towards the Royal Family. Within hours of the abdication, over 20.000 people amassed in Madrid to demand a referendum on the future of the monarchy. They were joined by thousands more in other Spanish cities, as well as cities across Europe and Latin America.

Adding fuel to the fire, the aunt of the new Queen-to-be Letizia - sparked an online petition in favour of a referendum on the day of the abdication. She tweeted:

#ElReyAbdica #ReferendumYA -- Es hora de que hable la ciudadanía. Firma y RT! +201 mil y creciendo...
(#TheKing Abdicates #ReferendumNow - It's time for the people to speak. Sign and retweet! 201 thousand and growing...)

Henar Ortiz Álvarez had previously described herself as a "red and a republican" and claimed in the magazine Vanity Fair that Letizia herself had held republican views before she married Felipe.

The desire to have a referendum gained momentum when newspaper El Pais, carried out a poll at the time and put the figure at 62% in favour of holding a referendum. The world looked on surprised. Wasn't Juan Carlos one of Europe's most popular Royals? Why had the abdication provoked such a huge Republican sentiment?

The recent Botswana scandal probably had something to do with it, but the final straw could have been the list of scandals that surrounded the royals - from rumours of the King having a mistress to corruption in the Royal household. So it was not surprising to see a push for a "a renewed monarchy for new times," as Felipe himself put it during his inaugural address in 2014. Yet this did little to recover the people's fait in the Borbones, as a week later his sister appeared in court on charges of corruption, adding to the long list of scandals that had started to hit the country.

Cristina de Borbón was married to Iñaki Urdangarin, who, with his business partner, Diego Torres ran a consultancy charity. Funds destined for sporting benefits and for children's activities went missing and appeared in accounts owned by the royal couple. The case initially surfaced in 2010, charging Cristina with 89 cases for money laundering and fraud. In Feb 2017 the case finally came to a conclusion and Iñaki was served a sentence of 6 years and 3 months, whilst Cristina escaped a prison service

but was given a relatively small fine of 265.000 euros. To distance
the royal family, the new King Felipe stripped Cristina of her title
as Duchess of Palma.

D is for Duende

D is for *duende*, a small, elf-like, magical creature. However, if you have come across any literature on Federico García Lorca or flamenco, you are more likely to be familiar with *duende* as a concept of the divine, artistic inspiration which gives the performer an edge, a unique spine-chilling effect.

The words "*duende*" and "Lorca" often go hand in hand. In his 1933 lecture, '*Juego y teoría del duende*', he referred to it as "*el espíritu oculto de la dolorida España*" ("the hidden spirit of the Spain in pain"), the pain which is expressed by performers, mainly in the South of Spain. "*El duende no está en la garganta; el duende sube por dentro desde la planta de los pies.*" ("*Duende* is not in the throat; *duende* surges through your insides from the soles of your feet.") This lecture, by the way, is as full of poetry and imagery as his dramatic work. If you speak Spanish, do have a read: beautiful.

I think it's pretty safe to say that the concept of *duende* is confined to Andalucía. In his lecture, Lorca cites the flamenco artist Manuel Torres as saying to a singer:

> "*Tú tienes voz, tú sabes de estilos, pero no triunfarás nunca porque tú no tienes duende.*"
> ("You have a good voice, you know about styles, but you'll never make it because you don't have duende.")

The closest equivalent to "having *duende*" that I can come up with, is having "it"- sorry.

Duende is a dark force and though as a concept it might belong to the Andalusians, it's a force which pushes art to a higher level. Lorca mentions it being experienced by Nietzsche and Bizet and appearing in most performance arts at some point. *Duende* is at the heart of the purest flamenco. Without it, there is no expression of emotions, no real emotional connection.

Flamenco, together with Lorca, is one of Spain's best-known cultural exports. Flamenco is, indeed, part of Spain's culture, but it mainly belongs to Andalucía. It was probably brought into Spain by the gypsies in the 15th century. They were the population most likely to feel the pain of pure flamenco, *cante jondo*. The gypsies were not welcome in Spain and the word *flamenco* might have come from the Arabic words "fellah mengu", fugitive peasant. (*Source: books4spain website.*)

Outside Spain, the *sevillanas* are often mistaken for flamenco. The girl on photo of the cover of the first edition of this book (me) was wearing a typical *sevillana* dress, with its characteristic polka dots. The *sevillanas* are songs and dances which originated in Seville, also in the 15th Century, which have gradually incorporated some elements of flamenco. They are much more celebratory in their nature than flamenco and often make a guest appearance in weddings alongside the latest pop hits.

Like all traditional music, flamenco has also been modified and adapted to appeal to a contemporary audience with a more modern taste. While recently deceased artists like Camarón and Paco de Lucía tackled flamenco in its purest form, others, like the group '*Ojos de Brujo*' ('Wizard's Eyes') have taken some of its elements and fused it with hip hop and other modern genres.

Federico García Lorca

Let's go back to the playwright who has made the concept of *duende* recognisable outside Spain. Just reading some of Lorca's work can indeed send shivers down your spine. The last scenes of '*La Casa de Bernarda Alba*' ('The House of Bernarda Alba'), the story of five daughters oppressed by their mother make my jaw drop every time I read them; the hunt for the Bride and Groom in '*Bodas de Sangre*' ('Blood Wedding') results in verse full of urgency and passion being spoken by these two victims of the "*qué dirán*" (what will people say?) or of "*honor*", that raw pride which can make people behave irrationally.

In Spain, Lorca represents passion. He was a revolutionary by accident - all he wanted to do was express himself in his art. But in doing so, he held a mirror to the Spanish society of the time, reflecting back women's repressed sexuality and the oppression felt by individuals in small communities which resulted in bottled up dreams and desires.

Although he could be a melancholic man (and did suffer from depression), Lorca was also extremely popular with both intellectuals and the general public. One of his aims was to introduce the public to the great Spanish classics through his travelling cart, *La barraca*.

Lorca's poetic and dramatic works are varied: from the more traditional poetry in '*Romancero Gitano*' ('Gipsy Ballads') and the popular genre puppet plays to the surreal '*Poeta en Nueva York*' ('Poet in New York') and his impossible comedies. The great Spanish export 'Blood Wedding' has a little bit of everything in it for all of us. A traditional dramatic structure (three acts) sparkled with a little bit of surrealism in the form of the Moon and Death characters. Lorca's surrealist work was influenced by both his trip to New York in 1929 and his friendship with two other great Spanish talents: the film 'auteur' Luis Buñuel and the artist Salvador Dalí.

Lorca was not killed just because he was a homosexual, that would be too easy to digest. He was killed by the fascists because he openly supported the left-wing popular front. His support was dangerous because he was charming, because he was popular, because his views on society and art were ahead of his time. For this reason, he was killed like many others by the *Falange*.

Lorca was killed on 19 August 1939, exactly five years after dating his play '*Así que pasen cinco años*' ('When Five Years Pass') in which the protagonist, the Young Man, gets killed by three mysterious men in black. The site of his remains is unknown: he was just another victim of the Spanish civil war. There was no moon the night that Lorca died.

In the early 2000s, the Spanish government gave permission to try to locate the remains of Lorca and other victims of the Civil War. In 2009, excavations took place in Granada (against Lorca's family's wishes), where his body was thought to be located, but no human remains were found. In June 2011, historian Miguel Caballero Pérez, told British newspaper The Guardian, that following three years of looking into all the evidence and testimonies about Lorca's execution, he was sure that his grave was located one kilometre away from where the excavations had taken place. The search goes on.

Federico García Lorca's poetry still lives in Spanish popular culture, thanks to the very strong aural tradition and the many singers who have used his work. "*Verde que te quiero verde*" ("Green, I love you, green") from his '*Romance Sonámbulo*' in '*Romancero Gitano*' is a well-known Spanish phrase from his poems; and those singing '*La Tarara*' as children will be pleasantly surprised as adults to find out that they can easily quote Lorca.

If you are interested in Lorca's life and works, I recommend Ian Gibson's biography which can be found in both English and Spanish. If you would like to read a classic Lorca piece, I recommend 'Blood Wedding' but for something a little bit different, read 'When Five Years Pass', my favourite play of all times.

E is for Euro

Spain joined the European Union in 1986. During Franco's dictatorship, the country had remained cut off from the rest of the world, so joining the European market meant opening up various doors to Europe.

Young people quickly took advantage of this membership. The Erasmus Programme became very popular: a programme whereby grants were allocated to students who wanted to study in a university in a different country for six months or a year. I myself benefited from becoming "European" and was able to study in the UK in the 90s as a "home" student instead of as someone from "overseas".

In 2002, Spain put away its *pesetas* and exchanged them for Euros, shooting up the cost of living as prices were rounded up to the nearest Euro. Spaniards everywhere found themselves constantly converting in their heads the new prices to the more familiar *pesetas* and even now, it is still common to hear people talking about the cost of things in the old currency, especially when referring to large amounts like millions.

For those who travelled often in Europe the benefits of joining the single currency were obvious: the inconvenience of changing currency together with its cost was eliminated for ever, as was the need to go through passport control in the airports. Except, of course, if you were travelling to and from the UK or other countries outside the Schengen area.

With the introduction of the Euro, the black economy surfaced. As the undeclared *pesetas* were in danger of becoming redundant, they were invested in housing and luxury cars. Whether this contributed to the housing bubble or not, is for the experts to decide.

With the Euro came the term *"mileurista"* (the one thousand euro-er). A *mileurista* is a young person who lives with only 1,000 Euros a month (about £850). That kind of salary of course, does not allow many people to leave home at a young age and so your typical Spanish person will still find themselves living at home until they are in their 30s – unless they get married first. While this had always been traditionally the case, the low wages now prevented the Spanish youth from following the example of their northern neighbours, who, (at least before the 2008 crisis began), were more prone to fleeing the parental nest in their early 20s.

European?

I suppose the Spanish see themselves as part of Europe. As the different regions crave autonomy from the Spanish central government, one could even argue that some Spaniards feel more European than Spanish (see Ñ is for Ñ).

In the 70s, as the country became more visible to its European partners, there must have been a sense that Spain was viewed as rather old-fashioned or backward as the slogan *"Todo bajo el sol"* (everything under the sun) became *"Todo NUEVO* (new) *bajo el sol".*

In the last few years, the Spanish Board of Tourism has worked very hard to pinpoint what differentiates Spain from its European neighbours and as such, has come up with a range of slogans to attract visitors to the country. Moving away from the famous slogan *"Spain is different"* used in the 40s, 50s and 60s, the slogans to advertise Spain have gone from those building on clichés, such as *"Everything under the sun"* or *"Bravo, Spain"* to the more audacious *"I need Spain"* displayed in 2010.

(If you speak Spanish or if you would like to have a look at the posters created by the tourism office, have a look at Patricia Gosálvez' article in elpais.com on 16/6/2011 *'España en tres palabras: De 'Spain is different' a 'I need Spain'.*)

Until a few years ago, if you travelled on the London Underground, you were just as likely to see a poster advertising individual regions (Cataluña, Andalucía, etc) as you were to see one from Spain itself. However, recently these posters have become more and more rare.

The Spanish don't take themselves as seriously as their more "European" neighbours. Following many years of performing badly at the Eurovision song contest, one of the funniest, most sarcastic acts I have ever seen hit the stage in 2008. Rodolfo Chikilicuatre, (*chiquilicuatre* means layabout, of little judgement) was elected by the Spanish public as the artist to represent the country with the song *Baila el Chiki Chiki* ('Dance the Chiki Chiki'). The song, written by Pedro Guerra and Santiago Segura, the king of spoof (see **Z is for Zarzuela**). It's a refreshing spoof of summer hits such as the Macarena which spread from touristic hotspots to all over the world.

"Dance it with Bardem,
Dance it with Banderas,
Dance with Almodovar,
Dance la Macarena."

If you want to see the Spaniards laughing at themselves in all their glory, do watch the video on YouTube. Unfortunately, the song did not make Rodolfo the star that Massiel became when she won the contest in 1968 but at least he didn't come back with "nil points", like Remedios Amaya in 1982.

Spain and the World Stage

At one point in recent history, it looked like Spain was able to play with the big boys. In 2003, it wasn't unusual to see Jose María Aznar, Spain's president at the time, hand in hand with Tony Blair and George W. Bush, during the planning and invasion of Iraq. The Spanish population was uncomfortable with this association and Aznar seemed to be coming across as being out of his depth. It was no surprise therefore that the Spanish blamed Aznar's government directly for the 11th March Madrid bombings in 2004.

When the bombs exploded in the train station Atocha, everyone was convinced the Basque separatist group ETA was behind the attacks. The Spanish public threw themselves into the streets to show their disgust at ETA's actions. By chance I was in Madrid at the time and was able to join the demonstration. The government in Madrid made travelling on the underground free that afternoon to enable everyone to congregate in the centre. Half of the city (according to Wikipedia) came together in the streets under their umbrellas, for Madrid was weeping that day.

But this solidarity between people and government didn't last long. On Friday, the Spanish took to the streets. On Saturday, rumours started circulating that it had been Al-Qaeda and not ETA that had planted the bomb in response to Spain's involvement in the Iraq war. By Sunday, the Spanish showed the Popular Party their distrust by voting the socialist PSOE into power in the general elections.

The bombs were obviously planted to cause maximum chaos three days before the country's general election. You can image the number of conspiracy theories that have emerged linking both ETA and the PSOE in some measure to the bombings. To research and relate all the facts would take another book so for now I will just say that, at the time of writing (June 2012) there are still many organisations and individuals who consider this case far from closed.

But I digress.

The European Union

So, has Spain changed as a result of joining the European Union? It's difficult to say. Certainly Spain seems to have benefited economically through Europe's regeneration funds, as the country has received more funds than it has contributed and has been able to use money earmarked for regeneration projects to fund up to 80% of its new traffic infrastructure. The civil servants have the opportunity to learn directly from their peers through reciprocal training and travelling has become a bit more comfortable for the keen Spanish tourist.

On the other hand, European quotas which limit the amount of products a country can export to other Europeans has had a negative effect. Many oranges have gone to waste because of this, for example, and so, a number of Spanish farmers growing oranges have had to relocate to Morocco and export their fruit to Europe from there. While upon joining, Spain was one of the countries in most need of subsidy, it's probably now competing for funds with all the new European members.

In 2012, in the middle of the economic crisis, Spain's relationship with Europe certainly changed. While waiting for president Mariano Rajoy to announce whether he would accept the bailout from the EU, many Spaniards were angry that another country (Germany) was interfering with their affairs. While popular opinion seemed to resent the role that Germany was playing in their possible European bailout, many young people left for Germany to find work.

As for myself, I'm glad that Spain forms part of the European Union as that allowed me to set up shop in the UK without worrying about visas, resident permits or changing my nationality. Whether Spain would have been much different had it remained outside the European Union is up for debate and speculation. The country was rapidly evolving anyway after the death of Franco, so it is difficult to know what course it would have taken on her own. We'll never know.

F is for Fútbol

It can't be avoided. Football is part of every Spanish person's life – whether they like it or not. It's a safe way of having a passionate argument with someone else, about people you don't really know and who can't really hear you, so you might just as well go to town with your opinions.

Some of the Spanish league teams are amongst the best in the world, there's no doubt about that. Unfortunately, the Spanish national team was never glorious... until 2008, when they won the European cup. And then, they did it again in 2010, winning the World Cup.

La roja

Football fever swept the nation. Goalkeeper and team captain Iker Casillas was referred to as an *"héroe nacional"* (national hero) on Spanish morning TV shows. *La roja* ("the red" squad – luckily the Socialists were in power then) became a symbol of the Spain everyone wanted to see: vivacious, vibrant and victorious.

The national flag began to fly again. No longer a symbol of fascism but of unity and success. The country re-conquered its flag and re-instated the pride in being Spanish.

The Spanish squad represented the country in all its glory: young guys, playing very clean football, persistent and gelling together on the pitch. To top it all up, when Andrés Iniesta scored a goal, his thoughts weren't on the pitch but back with his friend and colleague Dani Jarque, who had died earlier that year from a heart attack. As he celebrated his goal, Iniesta lifted his shirt to show a white t-shirt underneath with the words "*DANI JARQUE, SIEMPRE CON NOSOTROS.*" ("Dani Jarque, always will be with us.")

Unfortunately, Iniesta got sanctioned as the rules forbid removing your t-shirt on the pitch. Still, I'm sure the thrill of winning the world cup made up for that.

Good-looking goalkeeper Casillas, had been getting all sorts of unwanted attention from the Spanish press for being in a relationship with an equally beautiful reporter. Just after the match, that same reporter interviewed Casillas, asking the usual question of "How does it feel to be king of the world?" Casillas, speechless, could not but express his elation through a full kiss to his girlfriend, on camera. The country cheered at this metaphorical middle finger at those who had said he was under-performing because he was distracted by his girlfriend watching the matches in the stadiums.

Against the backdrop of rising unemployment and political corruption left, right and centre, the 2010 World Cup flooded the country with a new wave of hope. The story of this victory had it all: honour, pride, respect, romance, emotion and even the knowledge that tennis player Rafael Nadal (who became world champion himself just a day later) had celebrated the victory with his fellow sportsmen.

In the summer of 2012, *la roja* won the European Cup again, giving the nation something to talk about that was uplifting, rather than depressing. Unfortunately, the World Cup in 2014 was a disaster for the Spanish team and they didn't even survive the first round.

Sports in Everyday Life

As in most countries, rivalries between teams persist through the ages. Real Madrid vs Barcelona is bound to gather most of the country around the T.V. in a bar, leaving the streets of Madrid empty. The citizens of the capitals themselves are likely to be split between teams: Real Madrid vs Atlético de Madrid; Sevilla vs Real Betis; FC Barcelona vs Espanyol.

Sunday is more a day of sport than a day of rest. In the "old days" the second national channel was dedicated to sport with basketball coming second in the pecking order. Spain has always enjoyed good basketball teams, with a few of their players becoming not only stars but role-models of good behaviour. Many are the products that have had basketball stars as their champions, such as Cola-Cao (the cocoa powder by excellence) advertised by the late Fernando Martín and more recently the lager San Miguel, advertised by brothers Pau and Marc Gassol.

Tennis has also had its fair share of champions with the unassuming, hard-working and persistent Rafael Nadal putting Spain on the tennis map during the last few years. Nadal follows a tradition of long-standing tennis players such as Manuel Santana, Manuel Orantes, and the Sánchez Vicario family: Emilio, Arancha and Javier.

The range of different types of weather, the Spanish's love

for being part of the masses and a varied geographical landscape which allows the practice of most sports from skiing to wind-surf, all contribute to the Spaniards' love of sport. Even the Royal Family used to be seen as championing a sporting life. Prince Felipe (now king) took part in the 1992 Barcelona Olympics, as part of the sailing team and I remember staying in the same hotel as king Juan Carlos on some skiing trips when I was only seven years old. If I'd known then that I would be writing about him in a book, I would have asked him for a quote.

G is for Goya, Guernica and Greco

Francisco de Goya was one of Spain's most prolific painters. Born in 1746, he painted over 2,000 works of art, including paintings, sketches, drawings, portraits and self-portraits until his death in 1828.

One of his best known paintings, currently at the Prado Museum in Madrid is the *'Fusilamientos del tres de mayo'* ('3rd May Executions'), which shows Napoleon's troops executing the Spanish population that had rebelled against them in Madrid in 1808. The painting saw the light in 1814, after the French were expelled from Spain.

Goya was a court painter under the reign of kings Carlos III and Carlos IV and as such, he carried out numerous portraits of the royal family and other influential dynasties. However, his artistic work went much deeper than reflecting the Spanish aristocracy in all its glory.

Goya reflected the horrors of war in his series *'Los desastres de la guerra'* ('The Disasters of War') where he shows the effects on society and the individual of the Independence War that Spain fought against the French from 1808 to 1814. His last series of paintings *'Pinturas negras'* ('Black Paintings') shows a really dark side of the poet and contrast in style and content with his earlier work in the court. My favourite one, *'Saturno devorando a un hijo'* ('Saturn Devouring a Son), hanged in the ground floor of Goya's last home, *'La Quinta del Sordo'*, which Goya bought from the previous deaf owner. Like Picasso after him, Goya died in France, which he had made his second home.

I cannot talk about Goya without mentioning Velazquez, another great Spanish painter who created around 125 works of art. Like Goya, he also painted for the country's monarchs but his work extends beyond royal portraits, although his style was not as varied as Goya's.

A few of Velázquez's paintings dealt with myths and other legends, such as 'Las hilanderas' ('The Women who Spin', better known as 'The Fable of Aracne'), which was inspired by the myth of Aracne. Without doubt, his most famous painting is 'Las meninas', a large canvas that enjoys a room all to itself in the Prado Museum. I studied the painting while I was at school and the story behind it made me feel very fond of it. Let me share it here with you in case you haven't read it in an art book before.

Velazquez was painting a portrait of the King and Queen when their daughter appeared in the room followed by her entourage, disrupting the scene. The two meninas (maids of honour) stand to both sides of Princess Margarita, who became the centre of the painting. Next to the dog stand two of the court's dwarves and behind them stand two figures who were probably in charge of looking after the maids of honour.

By the door, there is a man, probably the Queen's aposentador (chamberlain): but has he just arrived or is he sneaking out?

Finally, by the door we see a mirror, reflecting the proud parents of the princess. Felipe IV and Mariana de Austria might have been the original subjects of the painting but they have now been demoted to a secondary role.

On the left, we see Velázquez himself, not smiling, just looking at us: what is he sharing? The cross you can see on his chest
was painted on him after he finished 'Las meninas', when he was
admitted into the Orden de Santiago: Who painted it? Some say
the King did, but we can't be sure.

In the same way as I can't exclude Velázquez (which by the
way, is pronounced "Beh-lahth-keth") from a chapter in which I
talk about Goya, I feel I can't end it without talking about Picasso.

El Guernica

Picasso revolutionised art and, like Goya, left Spain for France.
Like Goya he also denounced war and the killing of humans
by fellow members of their species in the world famous 'El
Guernica'.

'El Guernica' was created as a response to the bombing of
the town of Guernica in the Basque country. In April 1937, the
German and Italian troops who were helping the rebels under
Franco bombed the town with the aim of attacking its civil population. Following the request of the president of the Spanish
Republic, Picasso, already living in France, depicted the massacre in a painting to be shown in Paris that year.

The painting is a large black and white canvas (3.50m x
7.80m) painted in a recognisable cubist Picasso style. Picasso
didn't want the painting to return to Spain until the country
became a democracy again and so it was housed in the MOMA
in New York until 1981. It was then transferred to an annex in
the Prado Museum, the Casón del Buen Retiro. Since 1992, the

painting has been hanging in Madrid's Museo de Arte Reina Sofía, a public museum dedicated to contemporary art.

The painting is an emotive reminder of the horrors of war. As such, a copy of it hangs outside the UN's security council's entrance in New York. When in 2003 Colin Powell delivered a speech to convince the world of the need to attack Iraq, the copy of the *Guernica* was covered with a drape.

Picasso had wished for the USA to keep his painting safe until Spain became a democracy once more. I wonder what he would have made of this.

El Greco

There are a couple of paintings that have hung in my parents' bedroom ever since I can remember. They are prints of works by El Greco, my mother's favourite painter.

In 1576, the Greek painter Doménikos Theotokópoulos left Italy, where he had settled down after leaving his native Crete. Doménikos was hoping to become a painter in the court of King Felipe II, who at the time was looking for painters to finish the famous *Monasterio del Escorial* (a palace and monastery near Madrid). Unfortunately, Felipe II was not too keen on El Greco's art, and after commissioning two paintings, he did not engage him again.

Fortunately for El Greco, he found a second home in Toledo, which had been the Spanish capital until 1563. In Toledo, El Greco found benefactors and the freedom to experiment with his artistic style, a style which had its roots in his native Crete as well as in Venice and Rome, the homes of the Renaissance masters. During his time there he was influenced by the masters Tintoretto and Tiziano, the latter influencing the way he gave movement and volume to the bodies in his paintings.

El Greco created many portraits, focusing on the detail of the elongated faces and hands. He might have even created first figures made of wax which he then copied onto his canvas. This gives the subject of his portraits a strange texture. His brush-strokes were masterful and with one single vertical stroke over an eye's pupil, he would conjure up the image of a tear.

El Greco's work was mainly of a religious nature and he became well known for his elongated human figures and his experiments with colour and light. The colours on El Greco's paintings are strong and vivid and he manages to depict the light as if it were being radiated from the people themselves. Many of his paintings have Toledo as their backdrop, a city that has come to be associated with the work and life of this artist adopted by Spain.

H is for ¡Hola!

Many of you will have heard and indeed spoken this word: but did you know that it was spelt with an H?

The 'h' is silent in Spanish pronunciation, except in words borrowed from other languages, such as *hamster*.

Spanish doesn't have many pronunciation rules: you basically read what you see, so it's a bit odd that the 'h' has its own rule: it is seen but not spoken.

Why? We are not sure. This silent letter was probably pronounced in a similar way to that of the English 'h' up to over 100 years ago. Many of the words it heads used to be spelt and pronounced with an 'f' in Medieval Spanish, up until the 15th century. If you ever have a look at a classic Spanish text, you might well find some words spelt with an 'f', such as *'fijo'* for *'hijo'* (son). In the printed word, the 'h' was added to those words starting with 'u' to distinguish it from the 'v' in old printers. In some Spanish dialects, the 'h' is pronounced in a similar way to the English 'h', such as those you might hear in Extremadura, Andalucía and León. But the important thing about *hola* and the reason why it has been included in this book, is not its silent 'h'. It's the use of the word as a greeting. And the Spanish love to greet.

Go up (or down) in the lift of a hotel and you will easily spot the Spanish tourists: they will greet you when they enter the lift.

"Hola."

"Buenos días."

"Buenas tardes."

If they share the space with you, they will greet you.

A dentist's waiting room: everyone will say "hello" as they come in.

The Spanish like being part of a close community, sharing the joys and pains of communal life. If you travel on a Spanish bus, greet the driver as you hop on. If you pass someone on a staircase (or if you enter a lift), say *hola*. Sharing the space, that's what it's all about.

"Hola, ¿qué tal?" ("How are you?"), is a common greeting when two people meet for the first time as they shake hands, or give each other two kisses if it is a social occasion. You can also use *"Encantada"* (if you are a lady) or *"Encantado"* (if you are a man) - the Spanish equivalent of *enchanté*.

Hola, (which by the way, means "Hello") is not really used when answering the phone. When ringing someone's house, you are more likely to hear *"¿Sí?"* or *"¿Dígame?"* (literally "tell me") or *"¿Diga?"*

I know we weren't going to talk here about spelling, but you have probably noticed the symbols, ¡ and ¿ . They are just the upside down exclamation and interrogation marks which are used to point out the beginning of an exclamation or question. Quite handy. While we are on the subject, here are a few more tips on pronunciation.

There are only five vowel sounds in Spanish A (cat), E (elephant), I (ee), O (ostrich), U (oo). The letter Y, when used on its own means 'and' and is pronounced in the same way as its Latin counterpart, I. Other consonants which might prove challenging for the English-speaker are:

V – in Castillian, it's pronounced exactly the same as 'B'. Again, its roots probably come from Medieval Spanish.

J - please pronounce as an English 'H' and please, please, do not pronounce it as 'K' or similar in "RIOJA" - this should be pronounced "REE-O-HA".

Z - keep it light, think "TH" as in "THEATRE".

QU - when following a Q, do not pronounce the U. So, "*Que*" is pronounced "Ke". It means "what", very useful. If you want someone to repeat something to you, do not hesitate to use it.

I is for Inglés

"Me voy a Londres."
"¿A qué?"
"A aprender inglés."

Every young Spanish person will have been exposed to the English language at some point. Probably at school for a few hours a week or, more recently, in a state bilingual school, a new kind of school which is reproducing at great speed.

If their parents saw the value of learning the language at an early age (and could afford it), the Spanish will have undergone intensive courses in the summer, lodging with an English family in cities such as Oxford, Cambridge or York. If you are in London, you will find young Spanish people learning the language everywhere, working wherever they can and usually... hanging out with other Spaniards. London is definitely the worst place on Earth to learn English.

The Spanish enjoy a strange love affair with the English (*los ingleses*) or the British. Many Spaniards left Spain during the civil war and the early years of Franco's dictatorship. Most left from Galicia, in the North, which is relatively close to the UK's south coast. Galicia has similar weather to the UK: relatively cold and humid, resulting in beautiful green landscapes. Many *gallegos* made England their new home and never returned to Spain. If you meet their children, they might or might not speak Spanish and they will probably speak English without a hint of a Spanish accent. It is therefore quite ironic that so many Spaniards left Spain for the UK last century, while so many British are now living their ex-pats lives in Spain. During the crisis of 2012, many young Spaniards looked to the UK as a place where they could find work (or at least increase their chances of getting work later on by learning English) while they waited for the economic situation to improve in Spain.

9% of European immigrants are British so it makes sense that Spain has many hotspots of British tourists and ex-pats, where the signs on the bars, restaurants and some shops can be found in both English and Spanish. These hotspots are usually near the beach and enjoy pretty decent weather all year round, such as the Costa Brava and the Canary Islands. Although this should be great news for the Spanish local commerce, the popularity of the "all-inclusive" holiday resorts has meant that local bars and restaurants can no longer assume that they will take a cut of the euros spent by foreign tourists. The all-inclusive package gives tourists a place where they can just pay in advance and enjoy as much food and drink as they want in their resort. A cosy way of enjoying your holiday but one that doesn't encourage you to taste Spanish life and spend your cents in the local bars and restaurants.

In Spain the British are famous (or should I say infamous) for their close relationship with alcohol. This is probably due to the fact that they have retained the habit of finishing drinking at 11pm, the traditional closing time in pubs. In Spain, however, alcohol is readily available way later than then. However, the

Spanish will probably not start drinking till about 10pm, while, by that time, the British will have already been drinking for a few hours.

This influx of British and other European tourists started in the 1980s, when Spain finally became a place that welcomed freedom of expression. With the slogan "Everything under the sun", the Spanish government really tried to sell Spain as the holiday destination where you were guaranteed to get a tan. While the Spanish were still finding their way in their new found freedom, the Swedish tourists attracted plenty of attention with their topless practices on the beach. (I can still remember my Spanish history teacher, Maria José, describing how the Celts invaded Spain all those centuries ago, "so that they could have a look at the wonderful Swedish women in their bikinis". She did make history lessons fun...)

The presence of people speaking English became just a bit more common and in the 80s, a comic character emerged on Spanish television: Doña Croqueta. Many will remember this man in drag, speaking Spanish with an English accent, probably something never seen before on Spanish T.V.. This character, given life by the actor Simón Cabido (who died in 1992), was an American lady, wearing a big hat and sunglasses, whose innocence and use of the Spanish language delighted T.V. audiences.

Over the last twenty years, the links between Spain and the UK have strengthened. Telefónica has a strong presence in the telecom industry as O2; the white logo on a red background characteristic of Santander can be found on most high streets (they even sponsor the self-service bicycles in London) and

Ferrovial runs Gatwick airport and others. Maybe in a few years time, we will see the creation of a new tunnel, submerged under the *Canal de la Mancha* which now separates the north of Spain from the UK. Who knows.

J is for ¡Joder!

Unfortunately, it's difficult to have an 'A to Z of Spanish Culture' without the word *joder* in it – a very common swearword in Spanish. So this article comes with a small warning that the material might be of an offensive nature and of an adult nature – if you consider swearwords the exclusive property of adults.

Joder is a very common swearword. It literally means "fuck" – and it's used in even more variations than its English counterpart. It's used as an exclamation and has downgrade variants (or euphemisms, to be more specific): *jolines, jope* or *jopelines*.

In its purest form, *joder* can be heard as a reflex to pain or used to express anger. Our J-word can also be used to express how much someone is annoying you:

"*¡Joder con los plastas estos!*" ("Damn these annoying people!") *Plasta* being synonym of *pesados* (literally 'heavy' but with connotations of being really annoying) but it also means "excrement".

As a verb, it can also be used as synonym of "to annoy or disturb":

¡Deja ya de joder!
(Stop bugging me!)

This phrase is so common that it became the chorus of a popular 80s pop band called *Los Toreros Muertos* (The Dead Bullfighters).

Here is the chorus, representative of the kind of popular music flourishing in Spain at the time.

> *Deja ya de Joder,*
> *Yo no me llamo Javier.*
> (Stop bugging me,
> My name is not Javier.)

Toreros Muertos was one of many pop bands that celebrated freedom of speech in the 80s by creating their own brand of urban poetry. (For more on this, see **M is for Movida.**)

Another strong swearword, while we are at it, is *gilipollas*, which is a few steps up from idiot. You can probably imagine the satisfaction of saying this word, which starts with a very strong sound, pretty much like *joder*. The colloquial variation is *gilí*, often used by those who prefer to watch their language – as *pollas* is the plural of "penis".

Mind your Milk

Swearing, like in most places, is used in Spain to channel anger or sometimes, aggression. One expression which has always baffled me is *"Me cago en la leche"*, literally, "I shit on the milk". There are also a range of expressions about shitting on people and deities, depending on the size of your anger and the person the anger is directed to. (*Cagar* is the verb that means to have a poo, which has the comical name of *caca*.)

Scatological language is also prominent in the Spanish

swearword catalogue and is pretty much un-frowned upon. *"La he cagado"* ("I have poo-ed it") or *"Menuda cagada"* ("what a poo") are two expressions you will often hear when things go wrong. While we are focusing on bodily excrements to help us get through the bad times, we can't miss out on the equivalent of "shit": *mierda*.

Let's stay with our colloquial language, but let's move on to more pleasant vocabulary: colours. There are a few colours used colloquially which have unexpected meanings. *"Un chiste verde"* (a green joke) is based on sexual themes or innuendos. So *verde* (green) is sometimes used to denote someone or something a bit dirty in the sexual sense. *Verde* can also mean that someone is not quite ready for something: *"Está un poco verde"* (He/she is a bit green, still not ready). This is also used to refer to vegetables and fruit not being ripe.

Red, when used to describe a person, refers to someone with left-winged political tendencies, mainly communist as in *"los rojos"* (the red ones).

Marrón (brown) has been adopted into a noun meaning "mess". *"¡Qué marrón!"* means "what a mess", a mess caused by someone. *"Me he metido en un marrón"*, means "I've got myself into a mess" or into something really complicated.

Lastly, *"¡Qué pasada!"* is often heard when something is out of the ordinary in a good way, or in a bad way. *Pasar* means 'to pass', and so *qué pasada* refers to something that goes beyond the ordinary, an unusual and quite extraordinary situation.

Pasar de algo, means that something is unimportant to you and so, you pass.

"Paso de todo."

(I pass about everything. I don't care about anything.)

This colloquialism has given rise to the word *pasota*, someone who according to the RAE (*Real Academia Española,* Royal Spanish Academy) "is indifferent to matters which are important or debated in social life, frequently because they are hostile to it." A wonderful example of how the use of language has given way to another archetype.

K is for Kilómetro

Kilometres, metres, centimetres, millimetres… they compose the metric system in Spain, following the International System of Units. There is however, a special kind of measurement you might need if you are visiting a market.

Cuarto y mitad literally means "a quarter and a half". It is actually a unit of measurement in Spain and has its own entry in the Real Academia Española, as 375g.

Going back to our *kilómetro*, the *Kilómetro cero* is the one spot in Spain out of which distances to other cities used to be measured. The origin of all the *carreteras radiales* (literally, radius roads) was here. These roads were set up by King Carlos III in the late 1700s to create a way of linking all major cities to the capital, Madrid.

The *Kilómetro cero* is in Madrid, in the Puerta del Sol (the Gate of the Sun), which is a popular meeting point for both locals and tourists. It hugs the spotlight on New Year's Eve, as its clock signals the official beginning of the new year. (For more on Spain's Christmas traditions, pop over to *U is for Uvas*.)

L is for Laico

There is no doubt about the influence of the Catholic Church on Spain's culture, even though since 1978 Spain has been a secular state: *un estado laico.* The monopoly of the Catholic Church as Spain's sole religion came to an end with Franco's death.

Regardless of its legal status, Catholicism is still the dominant religion in Spain: there are a few public holidays derived from the religious calendar (see *Y is for Yo*), Catholic buildings still enjoy tax benefits and most of the religious buildings are indeed, Catholic.

According to a survey carried out by the CIS (*Centro de Investigaciones Sociológicas* - Centre for Sociological Research) in July 2011, where 2,475 people were interviewed, 71% of the Spanish population described themselves as Catholic, down from 79.3% in 2005. 2.4% considered themselves as belonging to another religion; 16.9% as non-believers; 7.4% as Atheists and 1.6% gave no answer. However, of the Catholic population, 59.4% said they almost never went to Church and only 13% admitted to going to Church almost every Sunday.

The Spanish tax payers can voluntarily finance the Catholic Church by ticking the relevant box in their tax returns (*declaraciones de Hacienda)*, giving 0.7% of their income to that institution, a method they can't use to give to any other religion. They can, however, decide to give this percentage to the NGOs.

Even though there is freedom of religion in the country,

Church and state have a close agreement which dates back to
1979, whereby:

> "*El estado se compromete a colaborar con la Iglesia
> Católica en la conservación de su adecuado sosten-
> imiento económico, con respeto absoluto del principio de
> la libertad religiosa.*"

> ("The State commits to collaborating with the Catholic
> Church to preserve its economic sustainability, while
> respecting completely the principle of religious
> freedom.")
> Source: *La financiación de la Iglesia Católica en España,*
> published by the Conferencia Episcopal Española.

In spite of the fact that only 13% of the population considers
themselves "Church goers", the rituals of the Catholic Church
are still visible in Spanish culture. Children still get baptised at
an early age and many of them, around the age of 8 or 9, will take
the *primera comunión*, their First Communion. Some of them
will go on to confirm their faith as adults, in their early teens,
with the *confirmación*.

Primeras comuniones are still a big thing in Spain with some
of the more laborious ones resembling a small wedding and the
more child-orientated ones feeling like a big birthday party. I still
remember that of my school friend Jesús, where we all got our
faces made up to resemble American Native Indians - not very
traditional, but a lot of fun.

The boys and girls taking their communion dress up in their gowns and suits and the family and friends are invited to a big lunch. These are also occasions when children (at least when I was little) were allowed to smoke a cigarette or drink a bit of wine. It was indeed during one of these occasions that yours truly choked over her one and only *Ducados*, Spain's black cigarette brand (thanks Dad, you saved me from a life of nicotine addiction).

The kids are the big winners in these occasions as the gifts received for the *primera comunión* often surpass those received at Christmas or even for their birthdays. In my days, the "big gift" was a watch. This is still the classic choice but I'm sure many are rewarded for taking their first conscious step into Catholicism with a tablet or smartphone, or whatever they come up with next, if you are reading this post-2012.

Many children will not go back to Church until they get married. If you want to find out what a typical Spanish wedding feels like, you just need to move forwards two chapters in this A to Z, to the chapter **N is for Nupcias**.

Amén.

M is for Movida

I was born in the early 70s and can just about remember the day Franco died. I was playing in the sitting room, on the floor, looking up to the small (or extremely small by today's standards) black and white T.V. where they were showing his funeral.

After almost 40 years under a dictatorship, the Spanish finally recovered their freedom of speech in 1975. The 60s had been tame in Spain (maybe Lerner and Lowe should have used this phrase in 'My Fair Lady') as the young people were unable to dip their toes in free love under a very Catholic, right-winged regime. So you can imagine the jubilation when the lid finally came off.

Madrid

Madrid became the hub of entertainment in the 80s as millions of bars opened in different districts of Madrid. Malasaña became one of the most frequented neighbourhoods – and continues to be one of the most popular areas to go out at night in the capital, with bars such as *'La via láctea'* (The Milky Way) still standing.

The artists took to the streets (in a manner of speaking). It was okay to produce popular art, through which you could say anything you wanted. Pop became less polite and less tamed. Punk bands emerged; rockabillies; a whole range of new bands and artists who just wanted to celebrate their freedom by making music – even though many of them couldn't even sing. As almost anything went, bands became very creative with their names, such as Kaka de Luxe (*caca* meaning poo) and La Polla Records (*polla* meaning penis). It was also during the 80s that Pedro Almodóvar joined artistic forces with McNamara to form a glam-punk duo. And it wasn't long before he became a recognised film director and revolutionary of worldwide fame.

Bars remaining open until 6am. Discos opened until later. Alcohol being openly consumed. Joints and needles passing from hand to hand. Drugs available everywhere.

This was "la *movida*".

Although it feels like "*la movida*" happened a long time ago, the word has remained part of the Spanish language. "*Qué movida*" is used when something goes terribly wrong or when an uncomfortable situation arises, similar to "*qué marrón*" (see **J is for Joder**). "*Qué movida*" gives the impression that trouble is brewing, that, indeed, there's going to be a lot of (emotional) movement.

Whether you liked its outcomes or not, there is no doubt that creativity exploded during the *movida* in the arts. It was now legal to show naked bodies on the screen, which gave rise to "*el destape*" (the "uncovering"). Tall, blonde, topless ladies (and usually Swedish or some other foreign nationality) became the most popular ingredients of Spanish comedies.

Crystal Balls

The early 80s also gave rise to the incredibly popular TV show *'La bola de cristal'* (The Crystal Ball). This programme was aimed at children, teenagers and young adults, targeting each age group by segments. Assuming that the older the person, the later they would be getting up in the morning, *'La bola de cristal'* structured its content to appeal to an older age group as the programme progressed. (To watch some video clips, visit the official site http://www.rtve.es/television/la-bola-de-cristal/)

The *electroduendes* (electric elves), were irreverent creatures who artistically portrayed their creators' political views. For example, the *Bruja Avería* (The Fault Witch) had a range of slogans including "¡Viva el mal, viva el capital!" ("Hoorah for Evil; Hoorah for Capital"). Although the form seemed to be aimed at young children, the high quality of the *electroduendes* (whose puppeteers had trained with Muppets creator Jim Henson, creator of The Muppets) together with their underlying themes were definitely of interest to older viewers.

'La bola de cristal' ended with a segment hosting the most popular pop bands of the time. In fact, the second half of the programme was hosted by Alaska, who with Kaka de Luxe and Alaska y los Pegamoides (*pegamoides* has no translation, sorry!) became one of the most famous punk stars in the 80s. (She is still going by the way, still featuring in Spanish culture). Nostalgia for what was an exciting era in Spain can now be satiated through the purchase of DVDs of the series or many You Tube viewings.

With the end of censorship on T.V., came *los rombos*, the rhombuses. To indicate whether programmes contained violence or sex (or both), the two only channels labeled the programmes with either one or two rhombuses, depending on the "severity" of the content.

As Spain opened its frontiers to Europe once again, Europe's customs and American products entered the country, including many more T.V. series and uncensored films.

What Now?

So, what might be the equivalent of *la movida* in the first half of the 21st Century?

In May 2011, the Spanish youth took to the streets in order to express their discontent with the political system and the official 40% rate of unemployed youth. "*Los indignados*", "The Indignants", began by camping in Madrid's Puerta del Sol. The movement soon spread through the rest of Spain's cities. Uninspired, unmotivated and unemployed, the *indignados* wanted to tell their politicians that enough was enough and things had to change. They camped in Madrid during the summer season and made their presence known through (mostly) pacifist behaviour. The freedom of speech enjoyed by the country meant that there were very few incidents involving the police, but it also meant that the core message got diluted by the range of ideologies, values and beliefs that were being represented.

The demonstrations and spontaneous campsites lasted for around 4 months and the 15-M movement returned in May

2012, just in time to condemn the actions of bankers and politicians, responsible for the collapse of Bankia, a financial institution which had been recently formed by fusing a number of building societies.

Bankia was rescued by a 24 billion Eurozone bailout fund in exchange for applying extreme austerity measures on the country. Former chief of the International Monetary Fund, Economy minister and Deputy Prime Minister of the Partido Popular Rodrigo Rato and other bank executives were part of a huge credit-card fraud that enabled them to use the cards without declaring their use. 12 million was spent over a 9 year period whilst the bank lost money and investors lost savings. He was found guilty of embezzlement and was sentenced in 2017 to four and a half years.

Many ordinary citizens who had shares or other investments in Bankia, felt like they had been manipulated into topping up those investments, while Bankia officers knew the bank was about to collapse. During the next few years, some of these citizens managed to recover some of their savings after successful court hearings against the financial institution.

In March 2014, just before the European elections, the political party *Podemos* emerged from the 15-M movement. "*Podemos*" means "we can". It turned out that more than 1 million people thought Podemos could indeed make a difference and in 2014, they received 8% of the votes in the European elections, obtaining 5 seats in the European Parliament.

The tradition of just voting for the traditional political parties was broken and the *indignados* went from being young people demonstrating in the streets to playing a key part in the future of Spain. (We'll come back to the new political landscape in the next chapter.)

I watched all of the above from afar, grabbing bits and pieces of information from online newspapers and trying to deduce what was really going on amongst all the varied opinions I found on the subject. So let's give Paul Read now the space to tell you more about the other *movidas* that took place in the years following the 15-M.

Más Movidas

Between 2011 and 2014 social protest in Spain took new and creative directions applying new tools from social media to wrong-foot the security forces and the Government. Firstly, the 2011 Occupation Movement managed to disrupt not only the normal commercial and policing activities in the centre of Madrid, but also the smooth running of Parliament itself. Secondly, the government became increasingly embarrassed by organised groups that resisted home evictions and the ensuing bad publicity that followed such events (in 2014 there was an average eviction rate of 95 families a day). Finally, new forms of social media were enabling rapid and spontaneous forms of protests. Elected officials were spotted in bars, restaurants or on the street and quickly small crowds gathered to publicly confront them on controversial laws and political decisions. A new word emerged that described this form of protest: *escrache*.

The Government adapted new legislation that had been

drafted two years earlier and a new controversial law came into effect in July 2015. The *Ley de seguridad ciudadana* (Citizen Security Law) was also known as *"Ley mordaza"* or "gag law" because its aim was to silence or prohibit different forms of protest.

Some of these proposals included new offences such as disrespecting a police officer or participating in escraches, occupying public squares close to parliament of regional Government buildings and causing "disturbances in public safety", taking unauthorised images of police and disseminating them on social media. Regarding this last point, Amnesty International quickly condemned the law, saying that photographing police was vital in cases when excessive force had been used.

Modern Crimes

In order to keep up with the times, a range of new crimes were created, from tweeting the location of a demonstration to joking about the royal family. For example, a woman in a town in Alicante was ordered to pay €800 under the gagging law for posting a photo on her Facebook page of a police vehicle parked in a disabled parking zone. She wrote: *"Aparca donde the sale de los cojones y encima no the multan"* ("You park where you bloody well please and you don't even get fined"). The police tracked her down within 48 hours and fined her.

Over on Twitter, a Basque magazine photographer faced a fine of €600 after uploading a picture of a woman being arrested to his social media account.

As another example away from social media, Rapper Josep Miquel Arenas (known as Valtonyc) was sentenced to three and half years for incitement to terrorism, insulting the crown and making threats to King Juan Carlos in one of his songs.

Despite warnings by United Nations Human Rights Experts in February 2015 that these laws would threaten individuals' fundamental freedoms and rights, the government passed the new law in the summer of that year. In the first 6 months of the law coming into effect, 40.000 sanctions were issued that included on average of 30 a day for "lack of respect shown to members of the society forces".

Virtual Protests

On 10th April 2015, in protest against the imminent passing of the *Ley de mordaza*, I (Paul) participated in the first holographic demonstration in the world. The demonstration was organised by *No somos delito*, an umbrella organisation made up of representatives from a range of NGOs, civil rights associations and social movements.

Each of the protestors uploaded an image of our faces to a website, gathered them together and placed them on holographic bodies. The organisers then projected our marching virtual bodies and faces carrying placards demonstrating against the new laws onto the streets of the capital and in front of the Parliament building in Madrid.

Although it was an imaginative and creative response to the repressive new laws, it was a sad reflection that the right for collective protest ran the risk of only being attainable online, rather than on the street.

(You can watch a short news piece on the demonstration through this YouTube link: https://youtu.be/AyXsVHJSk44)

M is for Menuda Movida

Although during the first decades of democracy there were a range of political parties in Spain, during the 90s and 2000s, there seemed to be only two parties worth voting for in the general election: the Socialist party (PSOE) and the more right-winged Popular Party (PP).

As they consistently failed to meet the needs and demands of a new generation, new movements were born. Those movements turned into new parties and in December 2015, Spain found itself with a hung parliament after the general election, leaving many to exclaim, "¡*Menuda movida!*" (That's quite a *movida!*)

There were two main parties responsible for this, led by youthful, charismatic ideological leaders who had emerged against a backdrop of endemic corruption, inequality and chronic unemployment figures. Some commentators argue that Ciudadanos and Podemos share a number of similar policies, and although this may be true, their solutions are radically different.

Ciudadanos

This pro-nationalist Catalan party was launched in Barcelona in 2006, in part to counter the growing interest in regional independence (which is covered in **Ñ is for ñ**). That year it earned three seats in the Catalan parliament. By 2012 this was increased to nine and during the snap election of December 2017 they won thirty six seats, making them - for the moment - the largest single party in Cataluña.

During the Catalan independence crisis, Ciudadanos rose to become the main opposition to all calls for independence or greater autonomy from Madrid and they have tried to project themselves as the choice of balanced reason in the region.

Ciudadanos' leader, Albert Rivera, defines his party as liberal in its fight against corruption, unemployment and poor education standards, while also adopting a more right-wing stance when opposing healthcare access for "irregular" immigrants or wanting to impose stricter limits on abortion.

Podemos

Podemos emerged from the social and political vacuum left after the Indignados and 15-M movement of 2011. In early 2014, at a moment of endemic political corruption, an economy in recession and E.U. demands for greater austerity measures amongst the poorest communities in Spain, a radically new political party grew under the leadership of political science professor Pablo Iglesias. (Those opposed to the movement often refer to him as "*el de la coleta*" ("the one with the ponytail"), because of his long hair.)

At the heart of Podemos there beats a libertarian ideology which believes that decisions should emerge from the people themselves. They fight for greater transparency, accountability and representation at all levels of political organisation. They wish to introduce a basic income for everyone, an end to corporate lobbying and corruption, better public transport funding, reducing fossil fuel dependency, stimulating local food production and increasing support for renewable energy resources.

Nonetheless, the idealistic nature of the party hasn't stopped Podemos from making the headlines for treating its own spokesman unfairly in 2016 and from being accused of corruption in 2017. But we're getting ahead of ourselves. Let's go back to when the birth of a new party promised a more balanced political landscape in Spain.

The Elections

In May of 2014, just months after Podemos had formed as an official party, they shook the political world by taking 1.2m votes and 5 seats in the European Elections.

The following year, during the municipal elections in Spain, Podemos decided against standing as a separate party and forged alliances with other groups. They were rewarded by successes in Barcelona, Madrid, Valencia, Cadiz and other major cities throughout the country.

At the General Election on 20th December 2015, Podemos took just over 20% of the vote and became the third biggest party in parliament.

As no party could muster a majority nor agree to form an alliance, new elections were called for mid-2016. Podemos believed that this was their chance to become the main opposition in Spain, if they could take just a few more seats. To this end, they formed an electoral pact with Izquierda Unida (United

Left), which had evolved from the Communist Party, to create a new alliance: Unidos Podemos.

Unfortunately for the young party, this strategy didn't work and the combined groupings lost more votes together than they had held as separate parties.

Elements within Podemos now called for negotiations with the Socialists, whilst the Socialist leader Pedro Sanchez refused to entertain an alliance with either Podemos or the government, instead flirting with Ciudadanos for a possible pact. Spain appeared stuck once more in a stalemate position, and talks began on a possible third General Election. Finally, in a bitter internal war, the socialists ousted Pedro Sanchez so that the party would not oppose the investiture of Mariano Rajoy and his government, now supported by Ciudadanos. A third election was avoided.

An Uncertain Future

Podemos failed to win the general election and to gain sufficient votes to become the main opposition party. Critics began to write-off the organisation as a spent political force claiming it had lost its momentum and that it had too many internal divisions. A very harsh view considering this very young party had still managed to capture over 5 million votes only a few years earlier.

The political landscape remains unclear. Though now consistently falling short of an overall majority and despite the endless public cases of corruption and injustice, the Partido Popular continues to top research polls (except in Cataluña, where they came joint last alongside the Anti-Capitalist party in the December 2017). It appears that in most of Spain, although a large proportion of the electorate wish to see change, they still remain loyal to the old parties.

If the last few elections can teach us anything, it is that for the immediate future, no single group will achieve an outright parliamentary success and that everyone will have to become more consensual, more understanding and learn to embrace the art of compromise.

Perhaps the question is no longer about which party alone can lead a future government, but rather which can show themselves prepared to talk, yet remain principled. In so doing, politicians may still inspire and articulate our hopes for a healthy and progressive future in Spain.

A Different Kind of Movidas: Corruption

It is said that corruption goes hand-in-hand with power, and if ever you were in need of a clear example of this statement, you need look no further than the recent political and economic history of Spain. Perhaps as an oversight from the dictatorship, or perhaps because standards were never put in place during the transition to democracy during the late 1970's, but until very recently, there has been little evidence of accountability or transparency at any level of Spanish society.

Cases of corruption have appeared regularly in banking institutions, town-halls, amongst members of the Royal family (as we saw in *C is for Corona*) and the term "corruption" has become almost synonymous with Spain's main political parties - the PSOE and the Partido Popular. There are literally hundreds of cases that have come to light affecting thousands of officials, but perhaps four names will be remembered above all others.

Caso Gürtel

The main protagonist in this case was a man named Francisco Correa, but anti-corruption investigators chose to refer to this case by another name: "el caso Gürtel". "Gürtel" means "belt" in German, the same as our protagonist's surname, "*correa*". Apparently, one of the policemen involved in the case had spent some time living in Germany, and he baptised the operation with the German name.

Correa has been accused of bribing officials in return for receiving favourable public contracts. Arrested and jailed by the famous civil rights judge Baltasar Garzón, Correa's actions have resulted in a complex case that moves in many different directions. (Garzón himself was later stripped of his judicial powers and removed from office on controversial grounds.)

The Gürtel case has been ongoing for at least 8 years and has brought to light a hidden world of corruption and scandal. Showcase Partido Popular Regional governments - such as Valencia and Madrid - have fallen to opposition parties in the wake of Correa's revelations and the documents that came out of a system of double accounts to hide the bribes and kick-backs.

Although Correa has only received one sentence to date,

there are still outstanding cases to be answered and it is thought the final judgement will not be made until mid-2018.

Bárcenas

One of the many figures that emerged from the "*caso Gürtel*" was that of the ex-treasurer of the Partido Popular, Luis Bárcenas.

Bárcenas too kept a double system of accounts. In 2013, the newspaper *El país* published copies of these accounts showing payments made to prominent party members, including Maria Dolores de Cospedal, Rodrigo Rato, two names at the very top of Government and one "M.Rajoy".

Bárcenas faced trial for bribery and tax evasion, but he was hoping to be able to pull strings due to his position of influence in the party. He even received a text message from Mariano Rajoy, the Prime Minister saying: "*Luis, nada es facil pero hacemos lo que podemos*" ("Luis, things aren't easy right now but we're doing all we can.").

But as the case continued and that support never materialised, Bárcenas began to talk. He admitted in court that he filtered illegal donations from construction firms in return for lucrative contracts and from these millions of euros, he passed back sums to Partido Popular officials in the notorious "brown envelopes".

In a desperate effort to avoid further investigation, party lawyers in 2016 instructed the head of I.T. in the Partido Popular to delete Bárcenas' computer hard drive 35 times before physically destroying it. Such actions would not be enough to silence Bárcenas. He continued to release more papers, this time naming a mysterious M. Rajoy as one of the figures who benefited from the cash backs. Questioned time and time again, Prime Minister M. Rajoy simply ignored everyone and even refused to mention Bárcenas by name. Eventually Rajoy was forced to testify in July of 2017.

During the controversial hearing, the judge prohibited the prosecutor from asking the Prime Minister questions about the financial history of the Party, as Rajoy had claimed he was responsible only for the political aspects of the organisation and not the economical ones. In any case, M. Rajoy merely denied all knowledge of any illegal funding.

Whatever the final outcome, it is a sad state of affairs that such a large number of government officials and local authorities have acted with impunity for so long. Many commentators think that, had Bárcenas not been left hung out to dry by his party, the case might have never have seen the public light.

The "ERES" Scandal

In 2001 the Junta de Andalucía, (Regional Government of Andalucía) set up a fund to assist workers that were being laid-off or seeking early retirement, by being presented with redundancy schemes, the *expedientes de regulación de empleo (ERE)*. The funds would be made available to companies that needed to make these payouts.

A few years later, the owner of a business who had received a grant from the Junta to build a school was taken aback when two individuals offered him an unorthodox proposition. If he gave them half of the amount he was receiving to build the school, they would make sure he'd receive further subsidies to deliver training courses.

This incident kicked off as series of investigations that led back to the ERE subsidies and it soon came to light that money was being pocketed from the fund by businessmen and politicians.

In February 2015, two previous PSOE presidents of the region - José Antonio Griñán and Manuel Chaves - appeared in court along with 50 other people, as part of the investigation into the misappropriation of €855 million between 2000 and 2010. As the case progressed, it was moved to the Supreme Court where the prosecutor has since requested 6 years in prison for Griñán and 10 years for Chaves. The case is still ongoing.

N is for Nupcias

Nupcias means "nuptials", "marriage". The word is more commonly used when referring to someone who has married for the second time: *segundas nupcias*.

The most common word in Spanish for "wedding" is *boda* and for getting married, *casarse*.

I think I can safely say that weddings have remained quite traditional in Spain, pretty much like in the rest of Europe. Although as a ritual, the post-wedding celebration has a very lose structure. In Spain, it's pretty much a question of turning up, eating, drinking, dancing and that's it. There is no added stress on the couple and their family to make a speech, remember to say how beautiful the bridesmaids look, etc.

The traditions that have remained in Spanish weddings result in more spontaneous behaviour. Expect a sudden shout during the banquet of *"¡VIVAN LOS NOVIOS!"* ("Long live the bride and groom!") coming from a table, to which everyone else in the hall must reply: *"¡VIVA!"*. Depending on the atmosphere, you might get variations like *"¡Viva la madre de la novia!"* (the bride's mother), or *"¡Viva la hermana del novio!"* (the groom's sister).

Another spontaneous cry which will result in a bit of embarrassment for the newly weds is the popular *"¡Qué se besen! ¡Qué se besen!"* which inevitably, ends in a kiss (*beso*) by the couple.

Being married or not probably doesn't mean as much today as a few decades ago, by which I mean that the behaviour you exhibit in public with your partner will be the same whether you are officially married or not. (Notice how I keep using the word "probably" – this is my experience and I'm sure others will have observed differently.)

As an example, I will tell you a few stories.

My grandmother, admiring the fact that my boyfriend and I were not thinking of getting married as it would make little difference to us, told me about the time she got slapped by her sister. A few weeks before getting married, she was out with her fiancé to shop for furniture for their house. At one point, my grandma missed her step and hurt her foot. A little bit in pain, she took her boyfriend's arm for support. Her sister saw this and slapped her across the face. How dare she exhibit such loose behaviour in public! An unmarried woman hanging from the arm of a man!

Things have really changed in less than 70 years. Physical displays of affection are extremely common in the streets between men and women and in certain cities (or in certain neighbourhoods, because the whole country is not ready yet), same-sex couples also feel free to show their love for each other in public.

As an example of how attitudes to marriage have also changed, compare the gossip that arose when my parents left for the USA the day after their wedding in 1968 (everyone was sure my mother was pregnant, which she wasn't!) with my friend Cristina's wedding in 2010, when the laughter of her one year old could be heard in the church, in Cádiz, which is by no means the most progressive of cities. Furthermore, in June 2005, the PSOE (Socialist Party) legalised marriage between homosexuals. Times have definitely changed.

What hasn't changed so much is the fact that many young people still stay at home until the time they get married. Especially when youth unemployment is high. Still, the best thing you can do if you need extra cash is to get married.

Tradition has changed in this respect: guests used to be requested to contribute to the *lista de bodas* (wedding list) and wedding invitations would be accompanied with a note informing you of where the list was held (usually at El Corte Inglés, the largest store in Spain, where it's very easy to exchange those gifts that are not quite right for you). Now it is not uncommon to be given the bank account number in case you want to contribute in cash. The average cash gift sits at 150 EURO per person.

I also heard from an old teacher of mine, of a more colourful way of collecting gifts in the north of Spain, in Galicia. During the ceremony, the groom would pass a bag around, where guests would deposit their monetary gifts. Why not make it explicit that you expect your guests to contribute to your future costs as a married couple?

So, what else can you expect if you attend a traditional Spanish wedding?

Lots of food. You might get the canapés even before you go in for the kill, the main meal. Expect a starter, one or two main courses, a dessert and a piece of cake. Wine with your meal and *barra libre* afterwards – free bar while you dance. A Spanish tradition certainly worth keeping. All in the name of love.

Ñ is for Ñ

It really couldn't be for anything else. The "Ñ" is a truly Spanish letter, not found in any other language. It's pronounced "eh-ny-eh". If you ever need to write a Spanish word with this letter and you don't have access to a Spanish keyboard, it's best to use "ny" instead of just an "n", otherwise you might turn a year into an anus (an *año* into an *ano*) or someone from Zaragoza (*maño*) into a hand (*mano*).

According to unverified sources in Wikipedia, in 1993 the Spanish government had to come to the rescue of the letter Ñ as the European Union was willing to approve the manufacturing of keyboards in Spain which did not have that letter in them. In 2007, the letter became even more legitimate, as it was approved as part of the domain names ending in ".es", Spain's internet domain ending. I even came across a Facebook group, called "*Movimiento para la No Discriminación de las Letras Ñ W X Z Q y K*" (Movement for the non-discrimination of the letters Ñ, W, X, Z, Q and K).

The Ñ therefore, can be adopted as a symbol of national pride as the letter is central to the words *España* and *español* or *española*. But Spanish is not the only language spoken in Spain. In fact, Spanish is also termed *castellano*, as it is the main language spoken in Castilla, a region in central Spain. It became the country's official language in the 13th century under the reign of *Alfonso X el Sabio* (the wise one) as he tried to unify a coun-

.

try that was housing a number of languages, including arabic, hebrew and latin.

Currently there are three other official languages in Spain: *gallego* (Galician) and *catalán* (Catalan), both derived from Latin and *vasco* (Basque), the roots of which are unknown. These languages were suppressed during Franco's rule leading to an on-going, exponential rise in nationalist displays once freedom of speech was restored.

Indeed, if you travel to Cataluña, you might see more signs in Catalan than Spanish and Catalan politicians often decide to speak only in Catalan in public. Most Basque schools now teach their children solely in Basque. It seems that, as Spain has become more integrated in Europe, her citizens have dug deeper and deeper to hold on to their regional roots.

The governments have facilitated this division. While the European Union looks for ways to unify its members, Spain is split up into 17 *comunidades autónomas* (autonomous regions) each with their own variants of the tax system, public health systems and legislation. Falling ill in a different *autonomía* to yours can be as cumbersome as falling ill in a different country.

The Spanish have always been a proud nation but now it is becoming more difficult to define what "being Spanish" means. Maybe that is why football fever swept the nation in 2008 and 2010 when the Spanish national team won the European Cup and the World Cup respectively. The country finally had a reason to come together bearing just one flag – sport heroes have the power of unifying everyone. As the Spanish flag had been a symbol of the nationalist dictatorship under Franco, it has taken a while for Spaniards to exhibit the flag without running the risk of being labeled a *facha*, short for fascist.

Just a few years later, however, the Spanish flag widened its symbolism. In Autumn 2017, during the Catalan referendum (which we'll come to in a moment), national flags started to adorn the outside of buildings as I hadn't seen before. While different kinds of Catalan flags started to fly in Cataluña, the national flag was displayed over the rest of Spain to signal the support for those citizens not supporting the separatist movement, as well as (I imagine) to show their opposition to the referendum and separatist parties.

A few months later, when I went to Madrid for Christmas, I was struck by the number of flags hanging from my neighbour's balconies. Apart from the few that appeared sporadically during the World Cup, I'd never observed so many displays of love for the country.

So, what is a typical Spaniard then? As with all nations, this is difficult to define. I suppose they are quite loud (or "expressive"), they like the outdoors, they like to eat well, they like to stay in touch with their family, they use the car often, they like a good wine... but only with good food. There are a few regional stereotypes too: Catalans are supposed to be tight with money, the *madrileños* (those from Madrid) are supposed to be arrogant; the Andalusians are quite comical... There is more than one kind of Spanish stereotype but there will ever only be one letter Ñ.

When Ñ becomes NY

One official language in Spain that doesn't have the letter Ñ in its alphabet is Catalan. The Catalan movement for independence hit the international headlines in 2017, when the region's government held an illegal referendum. Here's Paul Read to recap the events that led to the instability that followed.

The Spanish Constitution of 1978 offered Spain's historically diverse communities the possibility of forming themselves into autonomous regions with a limited degree of control over financing, education, representation etc. This satisfied the different independence movements of the Basque, Galicia and Cataluña regions for a while, but the independence cause - a cause that predates the Constitution by a long way - was always going to resurface at a later point.

Since 1978, the nationalist parties in Cataluña remained a moderate and largely conservative force, but by 2010 the new Catalan president Artur Mas, was elected against a backdrop of two controversial issues. The first was the economic crisis that had recently plunged Spain into recession. This was seen by some Catalans as one more reason why Cataluña should handle its own economic affairs.

The second issue related to Catalan legislation passed in 2006 that referred to the country as a "nation" and authorised the Catalan state to take greater control over judicial and fiscal responsibilities. This legislation was later overturned by Spain's Constitutional court in 2010. Artur Mas began to feel pressure from more committed nationalist parties to respond actively to these issues and so he called for a symbolic referendum on independence. To gather support for this policy, he also called a snap election in 2012, but failed to win an overall majority. In order to remain in power Mas was forced into a political pact with Esquerra Republicana de Catalunya (ERC) - the Republican Catalan left.

The Catalan government held their symbolic referendum in November of 2014 in clear defiance of the national government. Out of the 2 million people that voted, 80% supported the call for independence. After regional elections in 2015, Mas came under pressure from other parties to step aside, and he was replaced by Carles Puigdemont. This new president pledged to hold not only an official referendum, but if successful, a declaration of independence.

In August 2017, as tension mounted between Cataluña and the government in Madrid, 14 people were killed in Barcelona in terrorist attacks organised by a jihadist cell. In a momentary pause between national and local figures, King Felipe, Mariano Rajoy and Carles Puigdemont marched side-by-side through the streets of Barcelona in a statement of unity and defiance. It was, however, a short lived truce.

The Referendum

Carles Puigdemont announced an official referendum for October 1st 2017 with the intention of declaring a state of independence within 48 hours if the vote was successful. After a divisive debate, the Catalan parliament approved the legislation.

Immediately, Spain's Constitutional court suspended these laws.

As referendum preparations continued during September, police seized 10 million ballot papers and arrested 14 officials suspected of organising the ballot. The arrests sparked a wave of protests on the streets. In a clandestine move reminiscent of cold war politics, the Catalan government purchased 10.000 ballot boxes from China and had them delivered to a French border town to await collection on the 1st October.

With such economic uncertainty about the future of Cataluña and its trading position within the European Community, many businesses began to move their organisational bases outside of Cataluña. The situation became increasingly tense and was only momentarily relieved when thousands of extra police and Civil Guard were housed in the port of Barcelona on two ferries, one of which was painted with gigantic Looney Tunes characters.

As preparations for use of polling stations began to get underway, police were ordered to seal off the buildings and guard against their use for the referendum. In defiance, parents associations organised "Pajama Parties" in order to occupy the schools over the referendum weekend. On 1st October, as police attempted to close stations, seize voting materials and remove voters, the world's media recorded riot police employing an out of proportion level of violence against peaceful voters: Almost 900 people were injured including several shot with rubber bullets, prohibited under Catalan legislation.

By the end of a tumultuous day, the Catalan government declared the referendum results: 43 % of the population turned up to vote and of those, 90% voted in favour of independence.

The Aftermath

Two days later, in a live televised message from the King Felipe VI of Spain, blame for the crisis seemed to be laid unequivocally on the doorstep of the Catalan Government. Puigdemont responded by stalling on the promised declaration of independence, hoping still for a negotiated settlement. By the 27th October, the situation had reached a climactic point and the Catalan parliament declared itself a republic after a tense vote, boycotted by non-independent parties.

The Spanish government responded immediately by dissolving the Catalan parliament, sacking the government and invoking article 155 of the Spanish Constitution. This article stated that the national government was free to adopt any necessary measures to compel regional authorities to obey the law. The Government proceeded to call new Catalan elections for 21st December, appointed the Partido Popular deputy, Soraya Sáenz de Santamaria, to run the region and replaced the popular Chief of Catalan police, Josep Lluís Trapero, with someone less supportive of the independence cause.

Puigdemont and 13 of his deputies, including the vice President Oriol Junqueras, were then ordered to appear in court in Madrid accused of rebellion.

Election Campaigns

Puigdemont fled to Brussels with four *compañeros* in the hope of gaining support from the European community. A request for his extradition was made to Belgium on the grounds of sedition and rebellion. Puigdemont refused to return to Spain under such conditions.

Meanwhile, eight Catalan independence ministers were imprisoned. The Spanish government betted on an alliance of anti-independence parties to keep the separatists out of office, but the election held on 21st December 2017 failed to produce the result they had hoped for.

Although Ciudadanos became the most voted for single party, the combined forces of the independent parties won enough seats to form an overall majority. On the 17th January, with Puigdemont still in exile and Oriol Junqueras still in prison, once more a pro-independence coalition was voted into Government.

An Uncertain Future

Neither the symbolic referendum in October, nor the unilateral declaration of independence by the separatists achieved what they had hoped for. Neither the deployment of state police against peaceful voters nor the subsequent imprisonment of politicians has achieved what Madrid had hoped for.

Political questions, particularly ones that touch on ideas of identity and culture - will never be resolved in court, in prison nor with the use of force on the street. At the time of writing, we can only hope that dialogue, discussion and ultimately the ballot box will bring about a peaceful and lasting settlement to this difficult question of national identity.

O is for ¡Olé!

"¡Olé!" is often heard in flamenco shows after a particularly embellished sequence or during bullfights, when the bullfighter performs a particularly embellished *pase*. Although I haven't been able to identify where the expression comes from, it's most probably derived from the Arabic "Allah", God. (Not even Lorca was sure of its origin, as he mentions in his lecture about *duende*.)

Olé, toro and *flamenco* are Spanish words that many foreigners can utter, along with *cerveza* and *vino*, of course – as well as the bastardised version of "*sin problema*" (no problem) which has become "*no problemo*". If you like using that phrase, that's fine, it has become part of English colloquial language. As long as you know that in Spanish, it's grammatically wrong. Let me explain why.

Most Spanish words carry with them the feminine or masculine gender. For example, a house will be feminine (*la casa*), while the sky is masculine (*el cielo*). 'La' is the article for feminine nouns; '*el*', for masculine (and "lo" for neutral, but that is a matter for another specialist book). '*La casa*' and '*el cielo*' are classic examples of words that, ending in 'a' are feminine and those ending in 'o' are masculine. However, sometimes, this is not the case and this exception can be illustrated by the word '*problema*'. Although ending in an 'a', this is a masculine word: **el** *problema,* **un** *problema,* **los** *problemas.* So you can see how *problema* has become '*problemo*' in the mouths of non-Spanish speakers.

But I digress (a lot).

Los toros

Let's get back to the bulls. Bullfighting is not only one of many traditions in Spain, but one that is gradually disappearing. Personally, I've never liked it and when I was little, I would switch off the television when bullfights were being shown. Now regional governments have gone as far as to forbid this form of entertainment. In January 2012, they became illegal in Cataluña; whereas in the Canary Islands, they have been illegal since 1991, after a law was passed which prohibited all animals from being cruelly used in *fiestas* and entertainments. Some people are happy with these prohibitions. Some see it as the end of an artform, for there is something spectacular about it: the costumes involved, the music, the crowds, the *pases* as the bullfighter elegantly swerves his or her cape. There is even suspense and a sense of danger, as it is not uncommon for the bull to get his revenge by playing "toss around the bullfighter" with his horns. This tradition lies at the heart of Spanish culture for some and has been labeled "*la fiesta nacional*".

In April 2012, 590,000 people (out of a population of around 46 million) signed a petition asking for bullfighting to be declared *Bien de Interés Cultural* (of cultural interest), to try to revoke its prohibition. In October 2016, the ban was overturned by the Spanish Constitutional Court which ruled that an autonomous region is allowed only to regulate bullfighting, but not ban it. Finally, after being absent for 6 years from Spanish television, bullfighting returned to the country's small screens in September 2012.

Whether bullfighting should be banned or celebrated seems to be an ongoing debate in Spain, but one about which I don't feel passionate about either way, so let's move on to other popular fiestas.

Bulls also feature heavily in other celebrations. The most famous one is *Los San Fermines*, celebrated in honour of San Fermín, patron saint of Pamplona, in Navarra, in the North of Spain, on the 7th July and for six more days. Many people relive the danger their ancestors felt as they ran away from beasts by running in front of a herd of bulls for about 3 minutes down the streets of Pamplona. Although this is the most famous *encierro*, they are also common in other Spanish cities and towns. Like most Spanish *fiestas*, this event also features plenty of singing, dancing, drinking and fireworks.

A picturesque event that accompanies these celebrations is the parade of *Gigantes y Cabezudos* (giants and bigheads) which features figures made in the 17th century. The *gigantes* are eight figures of almost 4m tall made of paperboard, representing the kings from four different continents: America, Africa, Asia and Europe. These giants are preceded in the parade by five *cabezudos*, which have huge heads of over 2m round. Their pace is solemn and they represent authority. They are joined by scarier *kilikis*, who will deliberately scare the children and by horses, or *zaldikos*.

This chapter of the A to Z of Spanish Culture aims to introduce you to other traditional Spanish cultural aspects beyond *toros* and *flamenco*, so here are a few other popular celebrations which don't feature frightened beasts with horns.

Let's start with the celebration *Moros y cristianos* (Moors and Christians) which reminds us that, until 1492, the Arabs were prominent in Spain. In fact, to go back to the title of this chapter, one of the theories as to the origin of *Olé* is that it comes from the Arab "Allah-walla" (by Allah). *Moros y cristianos* takes place in various cities and towns in Alicante, near the Mediterranean, and they are particularly notorious in Alcoy.

Moros y Cristianos

My friend Fidel comes from Alcoy, a beautiful small town on the Mediterranean coast. It is through him that I learnt properly about *Moros y cristianos*. Well, through him and his son Alvaro, who very kindly shared with me the school presentation he did on this *fiesta*.

This *Moros y cristianos* tradition recreates a very specific battle that took place in 1276 in Alcoy. On 23rd April, having lost the city to the Kingdom of Valencia (Spain has quite a tradition of division, it was made up of lots of separate kingdoms until 1492) the Moors tried to conquer the city once more under the leadership of Al-Azraq "*el azul*" (the blue one), 'blue' due to the colour of his eyes. A bloody battle ensued between Muslim and Christian troops.

When it seemed inevitable that the Arabs were going to win the battle, a mysterious male figure appeared riding a white horse and displaying a red cross on his chest. With one blow, the warrior, identified by the Christian troops as St Jordi (patron saint on that day) took the life of the Arab leader, causing the rest of his troops to disperse.

The result of this important day when the Spanish recon-
quered their city is celebrated in Alcoy over three days no less.
This *trilogía* runs from 22nd to 24th April. The first day features
different music bands playing through the streets of Alcoy and
it ends with the whole town eating an *olleta alcoyana*, a casserole-type dish including pork, beef, potatoes, beans and *morcilla*,
a kind of sausage made of pig's blood and meat.

The following day's celebrations start early. At 6am, the
trumpet sounds and both sets of troops parade through the city
as the sun begins to rise. (My friend Fidel has impersonated a
Moor for ages.) A beautiful reconstruction of medieval times
ensues, with the Christian side parading in the morning and the
Moorish side taking over the streets in the afternoon.

The second day is dedicated to St Jordi. It consists mainly
of *procesiones* (processions) similar to those seen during Easter,
but featuring an image of St Jordi which is carried from church
to church.

On the last day, the whole thing explodes. Literally.
Gunpowder features heavily on this day as the battle between
moros and *cristianos* is reconstructed, showing the Moors victorious in the morning while in the afternoon, the Christians take
the city back.

Plenty of noise and celebratory behaviour then, but not
nearly as much as that which you can see in *Las fallas* in Valencia.

Las fallas

For the four days prior to 19th March (San José, the carpenters' patron saint and Valencia's), Valencia turns into a concoction of noise, music and smoke.

The day starts with the *despertás*, setting off gunpowder to let everyone know that the celebrations are about to begin. In the afternoon, prepare yourself to have your eardrums challenged by the *mascletás* created by extremely powerful bangers which are set off over the noise and chanting of the population. If fireworks are your poison, then you can enjoy what is probably one of the most impressive fireworks display in the world. *La Nit del Foc* in Valencia ("the night of fire" in *Valenciá*, the official language) attracts around 650,000 people every year at 1.30 in the morning before San José.

Finally, on the last day of *las fallas*, Valencia is flooded by flames and smoke as all the *ninots* go up in flames. The *ninots* are wonderfully artistic figures made of different flammable materials, such as paperboard and wood. It is these *ninots*, when put together to create a work of art, that make a *falla* which gives this celebration its name. The size of the *fallas* varies, from 5m high and around 25 square meters, to those under the "special" category, which can be as high as 20m tall and around 200 square metres.

Months of work go into these figures that surrender to their fate on the last day of *Las fallas*. All, except one: the competition winner.

You might be asking yourself: "Why?" Why do artists invest

so much time in creating these figures which end up as a pile of ashes? The answer is a common one: tradition.

Before the 17th century, the carpenters and artisans of Valencia would celebrate the arrival of spring by burning the holders which had supported the oil lamps used to give light in the winter. On the night before San José, they would burn piles of unwanted lamp holders and any other bits of leftover wood. With time, the carpenters began to dress up these unwanted items to satirise society, by creating parodies of the middle classes and the Church.

Gradually, this event became more popular and sophisticated and of course, controversial. After trying to suppress these celebrations for decades, the Mayor finally succumbed to the will of the people and in 1932, the Council became the official organiser of the event. The younger *valencianos* and *valencianas* now even enjoy their own child-themed *fallas*.

As in most Spanish festivities, seasonal food features heavily, this time in the shape of the cold drink *horchata*, made from tigernuts (*chufas*) in which you can dip your *fartons*, a wheat-based pastry.

Las fallas has become one of the most popular celebrations in Spain, attracting around 1.5 million visitors in 2012. Great fun for those wishing to party all night but not so great for some of the locals, like my aunt, who are unable to sleep for one week.

P is for Paraguas

It might surprise some of you but it does rain in Spain and when it does, you will need an umbrella, a *paraguas*. This word means literally that: stop (*para*) the waters (*aguas*) or, I suppose it could also be an object for (*para*) the waters.

It's not always sunny in Spain. It might be more accurate to say that it's not always sunny in all of Spain.

For Spain is quite large and therefore each region has its own weather characteristics. Maybe in Andalucía, for example, it's warm most of the time. The average minimum temperature in Málaga in the month of November 2010 was 9 degrees Celsius - but it did rain a lot.

Or take Valencia, where my father's side of the family comes from. In the winter it gets reasonably cold but you won't need your scarf and gloves for most of it. If you're lucky, you will even get warm, sunny spells. I relish Christmas in that region as it is not unusual for me to have to take my coat off when I go for a walk in the city. Inside the flats though, it's a different story. They have been built to guard off the heat and so their floors tend to be made of marble and they rarely have central heating

At the other extreme, we have Galicia. Galicia has a very green landscape - and that my friends, means that there is rain. Yes, it does rain in Spain. After all, professor Higgins (in 'My Fair Lady') was not completely off the mark when he said that "the rain in Spain stays mainly on the plain".

In the centre of Spain, the weather can go to extremes. For example, in Madrid the end of July and beginning of August tend to be extremely hot with temperatures reaching around 40 degrees centigrade at midday. By midday, I mean 2 – 3pm, as that is midday in Spain (not 12pm). On the other hand, in the winter, be prepared to wrap up warm as temperatures often fall below cero. It all makes sense when you consider that the city is surrounded by mountains.

The fact that Spain boasts of some high-quality, popular skiing resorts such as Baqueira Beret or Cerler provides a small clue to the kind of weather that can take over some of the country. Sierra Nevada is located in Granada, Andalucía, so you might enjoy some sunshine during your skiing trips – although there is of course always the danger that there won't be enough snow.

Q is for Quijote

"En un lugar de la mancha, de cuyo nombre no quiero acordarme..."
("In a place in La Mancha, the name of which I don't want to remember...")

El Quijote is one of the most popular figures in Spanish literature. '*Las aventuras del ingenioso hidalgo Don Quijote*' ('The Adventures of the Ingenious Gentleman Don Quixote') is a thick book written in two parts in 1605 and 1615, which forms part of every Spaniard's education. What's so wonderful about it is that it's a lot of fun and therefore provides an excellent introduction to the Classics genre.

The novel narrates the adventures of a mad man, of a gentleman who goes mad from reading chivalry novels. As he sets off on new adventures and those around him realise he's lost his marbles, they make fun of him, they taunt him. All except for his companion, good ol' Sancho Panza, who tries to bring his master back to his senses. He warns him that the giants he is about to attack are not giants but windmills for example, but even poor Sancho becomes delusional at one point and is taken for a ride himself.

The word *quijote* has become a noun, with its own definition in the RAE (Royal Spanish Academy): a man who prioritises his ideals over his self-interest and follows them to pursue causes which he considers just, but without success. The word can also mean a "tall man, thin and grave, whose character and appearance remind one of the 'Cervantine' hero". In fact, there is now even a noun derived from the word *quijote*: a *quijotada* is an action typical of a *quijote*.

'El Quijote' was written by Miguel de Cervantes. Born in 1547, Cervantes died on 22nd April 1616, the same date as William Shakespeare. Cervantes is indeed considered as big as Shakespeare in Spain. His works, which include both novels and plays (his famous one-act *entremeses*) are comparable to his British counterpart in both quality and number. Indeed, the works created during the Golden Age in Spain, which took place during the 15th and 17th centuries, still remain one of Spain's most treasured works of art.

Lope de Vega

Lope Félix de Vega, known as Lope de Vega or just "Lope" was another playwright who is definitely up there with Shakespeare. His plays were written in magnificent verse and had elaborate plots and well defined characters.

Lope's most famous play is 'Fuenteovejuna'. Fuenteovejuna is the name of a town which literally could be translated as "fountain for the sheep": *fuente* means "fountain" and *ovejuna* means "derived from sheep" (*oveja*). This town still exists today and the square housing its town hall has been named after Lope.

'Fuenteovejuna' is full of drama. Set in feudal times, the *comendador* (military commander) rapes Lucrecia, one of the town's women. After she lashes out (verbally) at the town's men for doing nothing to defend her, one of them kills the commander on his next visit to the town. In order to protect the killer, the whole population decides to takes the collective blame. During the scene where the judge asks the citizens individually who killed the commander, they all respond in their own way that it was Fuenteovejuna. The most famous reply is that of Pascuala.

> *JUEZ: ¿Quién mató al comendador?*
> *PASCUALA: Fuenteovejuna, señor.*
> JUDGE: Who killed the commander?
> PASCUALA: Fuenteovejuna, sir.

"*Todos a una, como Fuenteovejuna*", has become an expression completely embedded in the Spanish language. It literally means "All together, like Fuenteovejuna". What I have found interesting is that the most famous four lines of the play… are actually not in the play at all. A bit like the line "Play it again, Sam" in Casablanca. It's one of its most well known lines, even if it doesn't appear in the film.

> *¿Quién mató al comendador?*
> *Fuenteovejuna, señor.*
> *¿Y quién es Fuenteovejuna?*
> *Todos a una.*
> Who killed the commander?
> Fuenteovejuna, sir.
> And who is Fuenteovejuna?
> All together we are one.

Most of Spain's classic playwrights have been translated into other languages and enjoyed several adaptations and translations on the British stage. Lope, Calderón, Lorca and even the more obscure Valle-Inclán are household names in dramatic circles. There is however, one unsung genius who doesn't seem to have made it onto the world stage, probably because his language and jokes are so Spanish, they would be very difficult to translate. Furthermore, his plays are difficult to classify as they belong to a genre he invented himself, the *astracán*. The aim of this genre is to make the audience laugh, whatever it takes, using continuous jokes, even bad ones.

Muñoz Seca

Don Pedro Muñoz Seca was born in 1879 and wrote over one hundred plays. His most famous one is without a doubt, '*La venganza de Don Mendo*', 'Don Mendo's Revenge'. This play, which parodies romantic works, is written in verse and the quality of the language is admirable. The play has over forty characters, mixes all types of forms of poetry and includes jokes even in the stage directions. The play was turned into a film in 1969, directed by one of Spain's most revered actors, Fernando Fernán Gómez, who also played the title role. It has the feel of a stage play being filmed (pretty much like Olivier's 'Richard III') and is full of visual gags. The play was last performed in 2011, in a production by Tricicle, an established clowning company.

Muñoz Seca was another victim of the Spanish Civil War. While Lorca was killed by the fascists, Don Pedro was killed by the communists while he was in prison for speaking against the

Republic. He was one of those approximately 2,500 people who were killed during the *Matanzas de Paracuellos*, (the Paracuellos' Massacres) outside Madrid.

A tragic end suffered by a comic genius.

Contemporary Writers

So, who are the writers hitting the bestsellers lists today?

In addition to many popular Latin American authors such as Isabel Allende (Chile), Alfredo Bryce Echenique (Peru), Gabriel García Márquez (Colombia), Mario Vargas Llosa (Peru) and Julio Cortázar, the Spanish can enjoy the talents of a wide range of contemporary authors. Quite a few of them also have their own columns in newspapers and so are able to share their views and opinions on the world with an audience beyond their book readers. In this way, they are able to remain in the public eye even when they are not promoting their books.

Here are seven contemporary authors, some of whom have had their work translated into English. This is by no means a list of the top ten authors in 2012, just a list of those I think have a place in my A to Z.

Miguel Delibes

No matter how hard I try to describe Delibes' work, I'm going to fall short of praise.

Delibes was able to tap into the soul of the Spanish middle classes, of those living in rural Spain (e.g. '*Los santos inocentes*',

'Innocent Souls'), of children feeling left out ('*El príncipe des-tronado*', 'The Dethroned Prince'), or of widows torn between feelings of sorrow and liberation ('*Cinco horas con Mario*', 'Five Hours with Mario').

Delibes wrote more than 50 literary works, including novels, diaries and works of non-fiction (mainly about the countryside in Castilla, where he was born) and hunting, one of his passions. He lived from 1920 to 2010, becoming one of the few witnesses to an ever-changing Spain.

Alicia Giménez Bartlett

In 2011, Giménez Bartlett won the Nadal Prize, one of the most prestigious prizes awarded to a novel in Spain. Her winning novel was called '*Donde nadie te encuentre*' ('Where no-one can find you') and has a historical figure at its centre. The novel tells the story of a man who sets his heart on meeting Teresa Pla Meseguer, *La Pastora*, an enigmatic figure who emerged during the Civil War. She was part of the *maquis*, an antifascist guerrilla movement who made the mountains their home and continued fighting the fascist regime until the 1960s. *La Pastora* became a bit of a legend as she had a condition akin to hermaphroditism, which results in a person having both male and female physical characteristics. During her time as a *maqui*, she was known both as Teresa and Florencio and was eventually incarcerated for a number of murders.

Alicia Giménez Bartlett is also known for her crime novels which have the policewoman Petra Delicado (*delicado* means 'delicate') as their protagonist. These novels are light and enter-taining and reflect contemporary Spain while keeping you in suspense.

Javier Marías

Having spent most of his childhood in the USA, Javier Marías is not only a writer of essays and fiction but also a translator and columnist for the Spanish newspaper *El país*. He published his first short story when he was only 15 years old.

The first novel I read of his was *'Todas las alma's* ('All Souls') which is set in Oxford University where the author has taught a number of times. His prose is beautiful, blending past and present and managing to immerse you completely not only in the world of the university, but also in the psyches of his characters.

His more dense *'Mañana en la batalla piensa en mí'* ('Tomorrow in the Battle, Think of Me') is written in what feels like stream of consciousness. As well as being covered in romance, this novel is also full of suspense as the protagonist (and hence the reader) unravels the life of the woman who lies dead beside him on his bed.

Juan José Millás

If you are looking for something slightly surreal, with unexpected events and characters whose actions and words are difficult to predict, Juan José Millás is your man. Most of his work is made up of short stories but his novels have the same endearing quality to them. Who else would be able to get away with a chapter with shoes as protagonists in a literary work which revolves around the figure of a judge? The book is called 'No mires debajo de la cama' ('Don't Look Under Your Bed').

In 2007, Millás won the Premio Planeta, probably the most prestigious literary prize awarded by a publishing company with his charming autobiographical novel 'El mundo' ('The World'), where he skillfully brings the imaginative mind of a child to life.

Arturo Pérez Reverte

Pérez Reverte's popularity outside Spain is mainly due to his adventure novels set in the 17th century and featuring Captain Alatriste, an ex-soldier living as a "sword for hire" in Madrid. The "Captain" (for he is no longer a captain) features not only in seven novels but can also be found as a miniature figure, on stamps and in the 2006 film 'Alatriste'. The adventures of the Captain have been translated into 40 other languages.

Arturo Pérez Reverte's career in communicating with the public precedes his creation of this popular character. For 21 years, Pérez Reverte was a journalist working mainly as a war reporter. Now he delights readers with his novels and continues to express his opinion as a newspaper columnist. If you speak Spanish, you can follow him on Twitter under @perezreverte.

Soledad Puértolas

In 2010, Soledad Puértolas became the fifth woman to become a member of the Real Academia Española (Royal Spanish Academy). The fact that her speech focused on the importance of secondary characters in a novel does not surprise me: in her work she creates a world full of characters that stay with you long after you have put down your book.

In her book 'Cielo nocturno' ('Nocturnal Sky'), for example, the characters in a young girl's life weave in and out of her story: her traditional father, her left-wing uncle, a mysterious and well-known guitar teacher, her rowdy cousins, a "semi-nun" teacher (semi monja), a couple of school friends who grow up to be nothing like their younger versions and of course, a left-wing heartbreaker who turns the girl's world around. In this way and in the fact that it is written in the first person, it is similar to the novel which marked a change in her career, 'Queda la noche' ('The Night Remains'), which was awarded the Premio Planeta in 1989.

Camilo José Cela

Cela was not just a writer, but also quite a character. I remember him as plain-talking and as bold as the characters in his novels. I must admit, I only ever read 'La familia de Pascual Duarte' ('The Family of Pascual Duarte'), set before and during Franco's time, depicting the harsh realities in Spain. The novel does not shy away from the cruel truths of the civil conflict or the violence characteristic of the regime. '*La familia de Pascual Duarte*' was censored at the time it was published, in 1942, as was his later novel '*La colmena*' ('The Hive') which offered a depressing (if realistic) view of post-civil war Spain. This might seem a bit ironic as Cela himself had worked as a censor during Franco's early years.

In 1989, Cela was awarded the Nobel Prize of Literature, in recognition not just of the quality of his literary work but also of the boldness with which he had presented its themes and characters. The prize, according to the Nobel Prize's official website, was given "*for a rich and intensive prose, which with restrained compassion forms a challenging vision of man's vulnerability*".

R is for Refrán

You're going to have to excuse me. This chapter will most probably contain some odd examples of English grammar and some translations that might make no sense. It might even contain some perfect examples of "Spanglish".

For this chapter is about the *refrán* or in its plural form, *refranes*, those Spanish proverbs that carry with them infinite wisdom which goes beyond the few words making up the sentence. I've included their literal translations and some *dichos* (sayings) that might result particularly amusing in translation.

I did see at some point a couple of paperbacks in Spanish bookshops made up purely of the humour rising from the translation of Spanish popular phrases into English, so I hope some of these translations will make you smile. As with all proverbs and sayings, some of them reflect Spanish culture, another reason for including them in this book. So, I will stop "walking down the branches" [*andarse por las ramas* (beating around the bush)] and will begin with

R is for Refrán.

Más vale pájaro en mano, que ciento volando.
Better to have a bird in your hand, than one hundred flying.

If you compare this to "a bird in the hand is worth two in the bush" you will see that the "unsure thing" in the Spanish proverb is fifty times greater than that in the English version. Not only the number of "free" birds is much greater but they are also flying off instead of resting calmly in the bush. Could this reflect the Spanish propensity to exaggerate? [*Te he dicho mil veces* (I've told you one thousand times)] or to the perception that if you are not "caged in" (in a hand) then you must be off somewhere, flying.

> **De perdidos al río.**
> A favourite one amongst "Spanglish circles": From lost to the river.

The Spanish equivalent of "from the boiling pan into the fire", but again, much less confined in space than its English counterpart.

> **A quien madruga, Dios le ayuda.**
> God helps whoever gets up early.

Few proverbs still reflect the influence of religion on Spanish culture as much as this one. Getting up early makes you a good Christian and surely increases your chances of doing well in life. A bigger benefit than just getting a small bit of food, such as the incentive in "the early bird gets the worm."

> **En casa del herrero, cuchillo de palo.**
> In the ironmonger's house, use a wooden knife.

A poetic way of reflecting on how we often preach one thing while doing another ("Do as I say, not as I do"). I particularly like this one because it takes me back to the time when ironmongers existed and were respected enough to feature in their own proverb.

> *De tal palo, tal astilla.*
> From such a stick, you get such a splinter.

A rougher image than "the apple doesn't fall far from the tree". Can't quite see how this one is ever used in a favourable way, as it conjures up the painful image of a splinter...

> *Perro ladrador, poco mordedor.*
> Barking dog bites little.

The Spanish love their dogs, so it's no wonder they appear in their sayings. You will hear this when someone is making empty threats.

> *Del dicho al hecho, hay un buen trecho.*
> From saying to doing, there's a good distance.

Keep this one in mind if you have someone who is always coming up with brilliant ideas and projects.

> *Tirar la casa por la ventana.*
> Another example of how the Spanish language gives way to exaggerated images: "throwing the house out of the window", meaning to spare no expense.

S is for Sobremesa and Siesta

S is for *sobremesa*, that wonderful, long conversation that takes place at the table during dessert, coffee and over a *chupito* (a bit of liqueur) or *copa* (an alcoholic drink).

It is not uncommon for lunch to go on and on during the weekend. *Sobremesas* can become rowdy, especially if the conversation goes into any of the three forbidden conversation topics: football, politics or religion. The Spanish are likely to have strong views on one or all of these topics and unless you feel like having a passionate debate, they are best left alone.

Lunch in Spain can take forever and most people at work take two hours for lunch. You can still see this in most cities, where shops close between 2pm and 5pm to give you time to go home, cook a nice meal and have a siesta, our other 'S'. So, if you are visiting a Spanish city, make sure you don't leave your shopping for after lunch or you might be disappointed - unless you are visiting large department stores. This tradition is gradually changing in the bigger cities, but closing small shops during siesta time continues to be the norm.

If you are in a busy area, you will have trouble finding a table at a popular restaurant from 2 o'clock. Most Spaniards lunch between 2pm and 3pm and leave the office at lunchtime. It is uncommon to find Spaniards having a sandwich at their desk. Instead, you will find them in the bars and *cafeterías* which offer a range of *bocadillos* (sandwiches made from french bread), *platos combinados* (mixed dishes) and *menús del día* (daily menus). With a *menú del día*, you can have a starter, (or *primer plato)*, a second dish, dessert or coffee and a drink. All usually for around 10 EURO. Not bad, eh? No wonder the Spanish are not that much into snacking on chocolate bars or bags of crisps - their lunch provides them with enough nourishment for the afternoon.

The siesta

The danger of a big lunch is, of course, that it might send you off to sleep into that very well-known phenomenon called the *siesta*. Please, please, don't phone a Spanish household between 3.30pm and 5.30pm, especially during the weekend, as you might well wake-up the granny who has fallen asleep reading a book, or the teenager who got home at 5am, or the adults who need to catch up on their sleep or who simply gave in to that drowsy feeling that creeps in after a good meal. During the holidays, you are more likely to find any siesta-takers snoozing in front of the T.V. as the ever popular *culebrones* send them off to sleep. (*Culebra* means 'snake' and *culebrones* is the name given to the Latin-American soap operas which are popular in Spain.)

During the summer, the *siesta* provides a wonderful "filler" for those times of the day where you just can't get anything done because the heat is too much. Those out in the street will seek refuge in the stores equipped with air conditioning or in the shade; those at home will put the blinds down to prevent the heat from entering the house. To give in to sleep at that time is to avoid an uncomfortable time of the day.

Of course, S is also for *sangría,* that wonderfully refreshing drink made of red wine and lemonade, which can be finished off during the *sobremesa* and help to entice in the *siesta.*

T is for Tapas

Tapas, that wonderful Spanish export. It's interesting to note how a tradition that (allegedly) has its roots in the Middle Ages, has become completely exploited by modern culture and become a successful export.

So, what is a *tapa*?
Tapa means lid; *tapar* means to cover. One of the popular stories of how the tapas tradition came about gives the word this precise definition. Here's the story. (Medieval music, please.)

Let's transport ourselves back to the 15th century, to the time when the *Reyes Católicos* (Catholic Monarchs) reigned over a unified Spain. During one of their royal trips, Isabel de Castilla and Fernando de Aragón, stopped at a tavern to rest. Their enjoyment of a glass of wine was cut short by the large amount of flies populating the tavern.

"Please put a lid on this," Fernando said.

Showing his full royal respect, the man running the tavern picked up a slice of *salchichón* (salami-type meat) and covered the glass with it.

Another possible origin of the tapas as a "small bite", has been attributed to Alfonso X *el sabio* (King Alfonso the tenth, "the wise one") who, tired of seeing his drunken troops destroy every village they visited, ordered that all taverns serve small

portions of food alongside their drinks to help
drunk by the soldiers.

Luckily, this tradition continues. In most ⌐
will get a free *tapa* with your drink. (In some of them, ⌐
not be as lucky if you only order a soft drink!) This *tapa* usua⌐,
consists of a few *aceitunas* (olives), some crisps (*patatas*), maybe
cortezas (pork scratchings) or if you're lucky, some kind of pota-
to-based dish. In the most generous bars and cafeterias located
outside the touristic centres, the tapas might provide you with
all the food you need for lunch. A healthy tradition which many
other countries should adopt.

Ir de tapas (going out for tapas) involves eating informally
in a bar where, instead of ordering your traditional *primer plato*
(starter, literally "first dish") and your *segundo plato* (main
course, literally "second dish"), you and your group of friends
order a range of *raciones* (portions) to share. If you're not too
hungry, you can also order *medias raciones* (half portions). In
most cases, you will get complementary bread, a staple compo-
nent of Spanish meals. The usual times to have some tapas is
around 1pm, before lunch or 8pm, before dinner.

So, I hear you ask, as your stomach gets ready to rumble,
what are these *tapas* and *raciones* you speak of?

Here are some of my favourites:

world-famous: **patatas bravas** (brave potatoes).

Fried, square-cut potatoes with a spicy, tomato sauce.

The less exported **huevos estrellados** or **huevos rotos**.

A bed of home made chips covered with two or more eggs, ready to be smashed or broken allowing the yolk to flow over the chips. (Hence the name, the eggs can be either *estrellados* (smashed) or *rotos* (broken.)) Often accompanied by *jamón* (Spanish ham) or *chorizo* (spicy sausage).

Jamón (Spanish ham).

Prosciutto-like, but stronger in taste. There are different varieties (and therefore sold at different prices). *Jamón Serrano, Jamón de Jabugo, Jamón de Bellota*. Digressing a bit from our list of tapas, in the summer, you might be able to order *melón con jamón* as a starter, a delicious sweet and sour dish made up of a slice of melon covered with a slice of ham, for which you will need a knife and fork.

Chorizo (spicy sausage).

Best not to think about how it's made – just enjoy cooked in wine and remember that the "*z*" in "*chorizo*" is pronounced as a "th", not as a "tz".

Croquetas.

Wonderful croquettes made of béchamel containing bits of tuna, ham, fish or chicken. (Unfortunately, nobody makes them as perfectly as my grandmother, although those in the bar "El Automático" in Madrid come pretty close.) Be careful with your first bite, you might burn your tongue!

Calamares a la romana (squid Roman-style).

Fried squid rings. In Madrid and other places, you can have them in a *bocadillo* (French bread sandwich), also referred to as a *bocata*.

Ensaladilla rusa (Russian salad).

Using mayonnaise as a base, this dish may contain tuna, peas, boiled potatoes, carrots and olives, depending on who's making it.

It's worth pausing here to point out that many Spanish dishes are named after other nationalities, *ensaladilla rusa* (Russian salad), *tortilla francesa* (French omelette, for a plain omelette), *calamares a la romana* (see above)… and while we are at it, can anyone explain why the wrench is called *llave inglesa* (English key)?

Gambas al ajillo.

Prawns cooked in oil with plenty of garlic (*ajo*). *Ajillo* literally means "little garlic", another endearing translation. Be careful, they might also burn your tongue! If you prefer your garlic with meat, you can try *pollo al ajillo,* (garlic chicken).

Papas arrugas con mojo.

These are typical of the Canary Islands. They are small potatoes boiled in very salty water until the water disappears, leaving them covered in a thin layer of salt. They are served with a sauce called *mojo* which can be either red or green. The red *mojo picante* (spicy mojo) is made mainly from paprika whereas the green *mojo* (*mojo verde*) is made with coriander.

Paella.

Paella is mainly consumed as a main dish but you can also have a *tapa* or a *ración*. It is another of Spain's most popular and mispronounced exports. The double 'l' in *paella* (or *ll - elle,* as it was called when it enjoyed the privilege of being a letter on its own) has a sound similar to "y" in English, like in the first consonant in "yesterday".

Traditional paella consists mainly of rice, vegetables and meat and takes its name from the large, typical pan in which it is made: *la paella.* The *paella valenciana* or *arroz valenciano* (Valencian rice) has given rise to many variations in other

Spanish regions and households, not to mention the number of unpalatable versions you can find abroad. Some of the variations have become official and are expected from dishes consumed in some Valencian towns. For example, in Benicarló, they will add artichokes, while in L'Albufera instead of chicken or rabbit, they will use duck.

A *paella valenciana* can only carry that name if it has the ten ingredients which give it its Protected Geographical Status (its *Denominación de Origen*) which it has enjoyed since 2011, although it can still claim its name if the variations are along the lines of those mentioned above.

So, how do you know if you are eating the "real thing"? A *paella valenciana* will have rice, oil, chicken, rabbit, tomato, water, salt, saffron, *ferraura* (a type of green bean) and *garrofó*, a type of white kidney bean. However, the Spanish are far from purist in this respect and the *paella mixta* ("mixed" paella, with both meat and fish) or the *paella de mariscos* (with seafood) are also popular.

If you are more of a fish person or are not too keen on rice, you might want to try the *fideuá*, which is a fishy version of the paella-style rice *arroz abanda*, but made with pasta (*chifferini*) as its base. This dish originated in the city of Gandía, where I spent many a happy childhood moment as it's my father's home-town. The *fideúa* contains fish such as monkfish (*rape*), various mollusks like cuttlefish (*sepia*) and shellfish such as prawns (*langostinos*).

The urban myth extended in the Internet about the origin of the *fideúa* (possible thanks to Wikipedia) is that it was invented by a ship's cook in the 1930s, who usually cooked *arroz abanda* for the crew. As the Captain was a greedy man who often ate much more than the rest of his men, the cook decided to change the main ingredient of the dish to pasta, hoping that the Captain would eat less and leave more food for the rest of the crew. Unfortunately, the Captain liked this new version just as much as the old one and it was soon adopted throughout the port.

Though this is an unverified tale, it is a much more romantic one than the one I'd always heard: that the *fideuá* was invented by someone who had no rice in stock but plenty of *fideos (chifferini* pasta). In any case, the best experience for eating either *paella* or *fideuá*, is to sit around the *paella* with your fork and eat directly from the pan - but first use a wooden spoon to scrape the grains of rice that have become crispy and stuck to the pan. They are my favourite bits: the *agarraet*. (Which comes from *agarrado,* that which has stuck.)

¡Qué aproveche!

U is for Uvas

31st December.
23:59 hrs.

The whole family is gathered around the table. Grandmother, aunts, uncles, nieces, nephews, grandfather, grandchildren... All waiting in suspense. The T.V. is blasting: two T.V. presenters stand in front of the *Puerta del Sol* in Madrid, waiting for the clock to strike the first
DONG!
to eat the first of 12 grapes.

Eating *las uvas*, the grapes, is one of the most popular Spanish traditions: welcoming the new year by eating one grape at a chime. This takes great skill and preparation and each person adapts their tradition to suit their needs. Some people prefer their *uvas peladas* (peeled), others remove the *pites* (stones); others, like myself, cut them in half to help the process, although it does feel a bit like cheating, eating only half a grape per month. (I imagine that each chime stands for each month of the year to come.) Given the urgency with which the grapes must be eaten, you can imagine that more than one Spaniard will begin the new year with bits of grape stuck down their windpipe.

No-one is sure of the origins of this tradition, which is referred to as *las campanadas,* the chimes. The most popular explanation was that there was a particularly good grape harvest during the first decade of the 20th century, when abundant grapes led to their distribution countrywide.

Other sources however, say that it was precisely a scarcity of food that left the Spanish households unable to afford more than one grape per person.

There is also a third explanation (I'm sure there are many more in fact): that the lower classes in the 1800s, fed up of watching the upper classes stuff themselves with grapes and *cava*, took to the streets and in mockery, ate their grapes "in style", one by one.

In any case, things have certainly changed since then. You can now buy the grapes neatly peeled in a can, marketed as *uvas de la suerte* (grapes for luck, lucky grapes) – an expensive alternative to the already overpriced fresh grapes, as the price of all typical Christmas food goes up during the festive season.

Las campanadas

Families take their cue from glamorous television presenters. "Who will present *las uvas* this year, who?" "On what channel shall we watch *las campanadas*?" A big change since they were first broadcast in 1962 on the only TV channel, TVE 1, now known as *La primera* (The First).

"What will be the first advert of the year?" "Which variety-style show shall we watch?" (Again, plenty of channels to choose from, but most stay with *La primera*, for tradition's sake.) For a number of years, the comedy duo (formerly a trio) *Martes y Trece* would create a show to be broadcast over the last hour of the year. It was outrageous and it was hilarious and their work has stood the test of time. (*Martes y Trece* refers to Tuesday 13th, the equivalent of the Anglo-Saxon Friday 13th.)

It is important to train the uninitiated in the art of grape-taking. Many new to the tradition will attempt to take their first grape during the *cuartos* (quarters), the fast chimes that warn us that we are just 15 seconds away from our "moment". (Don't worry, Kevin, with time you'll learn.)

The 12 grapes end the opulent dinner on the 31st December, after which the whole young(ish) population goes out into the streets and into their cars. Expect traffic jams from 12.30 am if you drive into any city centre on the first morning of the year.

Different households celebrate Christmas and New Year in different ways. Many involve out-of-tune carol singing, accompanied by sounds from anisette bottles and *zambombas*, a cheap instrument traditionally played by shepherds that makes a characteristic sound.

Día de reyes

Decorations might include a Christmas tree and in the most traditional households, they will include a *Belén*, named after the town of Bethlehem. This is a display of small figures representing the Birth of Christ, though out in the streets, you will find much larger versions. Baby Jesus, Mary, Joseph, an ox, a mule, the Angel, shepherds, cows and some Disney figure playing a cameo role.

And of course, *los tres reyes magos* (the three wise men, literal translation "the three magic kings"), placed far, far away from the manger in the early days of December and getting closer every day, until they stand next to the Baby on the Twelfth Night – *La noche de reyes.*

Reyes (short for *día de reyes* (the Day of the Kings)) is a big thing in Spain. Many children will attend the *cabalgata* on the evening of the 5th January, a parade organised by the city council, to celebrate the arrival of the three kings bearing their gifts to Jesus.

Most towns and cities will have a *cabalgata* and if not, you can watch one on T.V.. *Melchor, Gaspar y Baltasar*: almost every child is bound to have a favourite king.

Children wake up on the morning of the 6th January (a public holiday, the kids must enjoy their toys for at least one day) to discover whether the kings brought them toys if they'd been good, or coal if they'd been bad –though those with a sweet tooth might welcome *carbón dulce* (sweet coal). Meanwhile, bakeries across Spain are busy making their *roscón de reyes,* a large, doughnut-shape sponge cake that hides within it a small "surprise", usually a small plastic figure which might land someone on the dentist's chair. Some *roscones* are a bit plain, and therefore a bit dry, but a hot chocolate or coffee can fix that. More contemporary variations include those *rellenos de nata o chocolate* (filled with cream or chocolate.) The perfect way to end the calorie-filled festive season.

V is for Vino

Like tapas, flamenco and bullfighting, Spain's wines are famous and sought out all over the world. For example, 60% of the wine produced by the Marqués de Riscal cellars is exported to over 100 countries.

Wine (*vino*) forms part of most people's everyday lives in one form or another. It is not uncommon to give a child a *vino con gaseosa* (red wine with soda) or, to call it by its more lyrical name, *tinto de verano* (summer red). It is not uncommon for teenagers or young people to enjoy *calimocho* (or *kalimotxo* in its native spelling), a mixture of wine and cola which originated in the Basque country. And it is not uncommon to find an open bottle of wine in the kitchen from which you can pour yourself a small quantity (a *chato*) of wine every night. (By the way, *tinto* is a colour similar to red, but deeper and with hints of purple. The literal translation for red is *rojo* but there is no such thing as *vino rojo*.)

For a couple of euros, you can buy a good bottle of wine in a supermarket – just make sure it's not too cheap as it can turn out *peleón* (fighter), a bit hard on the palate. For even less, you can buy a carton of Don Simón. Don Simón is a long-standing brand that makes mainly juices and wine-based drinks. Its red wine is usually used to make sangria but you can also purchase rose and white wine from that label. Furthermore, Don Simón now sell four types of *tinto de verano*: one made of red wine mixed with

soda, one mixed with lemon and their two non-alcoholic variations, as well as *sangría* in its traditional form, a sparkling variety
and an alcohol-free one.

The *bodegas* (cellars) where wine is made and kept have
become even more big business recently, organising tours for
tourists and wine-tasting events. One of Spain's oldest and most
revered wine-makers, Marqués de Riscal, have even opened
a hotel and a school for the next generation of wine-makers. Opened in 2006, the hotel, which incorporates a spa, was
designed by Canadian architect Frank Gehry, responsible also
for Bilbao's first class museum, the Guggenheim.

Gehry not only agreed to build a hotel that reflected Marqués
de Riscal's innovative outlook, but also gave his name to a red
wine selection. The Gehry Selection 2001 is made mainly from
grapes of the *tempranillo* variety, picked from a range of wines
over 40 years old.

Tempranillo means "a little bit early" and so it follows that
the *tempranillo* grapes ripen a few weeks before all their other
grape friends, such as *graciano* and *monastrell*. There are a range
of red wine varieties, depending on how long the wine is left in
the casket to ferment and how long it's kept in the bottle before
it's ready to be sold. Wines of the *crianza* variety are kept 6 – 12
months in the barrel and at least 3 years in the bottle. The *reserva*
variety is kept at least 1 year in the barrel and 4 years in storage.
Finally, the most expensive variety, *Gran Reserva*, is kept for at
least 2 years in the barrel and 6 years in storage. The older the
wine, the better the taste.

White wine is also popular in Spain and it is the main wine

produced in areas such as Rueda. Rose wines are also produced in Spain by mixing red and white grapes. Valdepeñas in Ciudad Real produces mainly wine of this kind.

Another type of wine made from white grapes is *moscatel*, a sweet wine produced mainly in the south and southeast coast, in Levante. There is also a popular juice called *mosto*, also squeezed out of the moscatel grape.

We can't finish our wine-tour through Spain without mentioning *cava*, Spain's answer to France's champagne. *Cava* is a sparkling white wine originated in Cataluña that can now be legally produced in seven other regions. It's the favourite product through which some Spaniards express their disagreement with the way Cataluña seems to have been favoured by the government in recent years. At different points in time, mainly during Christmas, you might hear those in other regions boycotting Catalan *cava* and deliberately buying a celebratory drink bottled somewhere else.

There are a few strong *cava* brands in Spain which always compete over Christmas to create the most lavish adverts and to attract the biggest stars such as Kim Basinger, Gwyneth Paltrow and of course, Spain's own Antonio Banderas.

To finish this chapter on wine, here are some tips on how to choose wine at your table. (Advice adapted from *vinos-ymas-vino.com*.)

If you are ordering white, pick a wine from the same year or the year before.

The same goes for rosé.

If you are choosing red, first you will need to identify which grape or grape mixture you prefer. If you are looking for a wine for a group made up of people who love wine in different ways, pick a *crianza*, as this will tend to satisfy most.

¡Salud!

W is for W.C.

… and for not much else. At the moment, there are only 11 words starting with the letter 'w' and they are all of Germanic or Anglo-Saxon origin. Most words which used to start with a 'w' now being with a 'v', such as "waltz" which is now *vals*. One oddity is the word "whisky", which has been turned into *güiski*.

W.C. is obviously not a Spanish word, but the abbreviation of "water closet" is still seen on some signs and doors to toilets. This word has been transformed into *bater*, which is the common word for toilet. *Retrete* is an unusually sounding name for a toilet, but it can't compete in elegance with *inodoro*. *Inodoro* literally means "without smell", and so, the toilet, as the vehicle which removes bad smells by directing our excrements to the sewage systems, has also acquired that name.

The toilet is also sometimes referred to as *el excusado* (which means "excused") and colloquially you might also hear *"voy al sitio"* ("I'm going to the place").

There's not much to say about toilets in Spain unfortunately (or maybe, fortunately). It used to be the case that public toilets were always a mess and dirty, but this has really changed with time. It is also not uncommon to go into a bar to use the toilet, if you are caught out in the street when you need to go.

Bathrooms in Spain tend to have a bath/shower, a toilet and a bidet and are fully tiled. Not much more to say about toilets and bathrooms – they are as uninspiring as the letter W itself.

X is for Xenofobia

For many years in the last century, the only role foreigners played in Spain was that of tourists. Opening the doors of the country after Franco's death meant opening the country to people from alien cultures, from cultures that had been completely absent from Spain for a long time. The government tried to prepare the population with a publicity campaign:

> *"España es simpatía. Sea amable con los turistas. Es fácil porque somos así."*
> ("Spain is friendliness. Be kind to tourists. It's easy because we are made that way".)

Widespread immigration is quite a new phenomenon in Spain. In the 1980s, it was rare to see people in the streets who were not white. I went to a school with an international student population and even there, I can safely say that the number of people from other races was around 30, not more.

The expulsion of the Jews in 1492 as well as the persecution of all non-Catholics by the Spanish Inquisition, together with the more recent dictatorship must have contributed to the lack of ethnic diversity in Spain at the end of the 20th century.

Things have changed enormously since then. In 2010, out of a population of 46 million, 12% were foreign residents, including nationals from the European Union. Morocco was the country of origin of most non-EU residents (29%) followed by Ecuador (14%), Colombia (8.5%) and China (6%). The list of immigrants from the EU is topped by the Rumanians (35%) followed by the UK (9%) and Italians (7%). In 2005, the number of legal immigrants was around 2.7 million. By 2009 it had risen to 4.7 million.

This new diversity in the population can be observed in the streets of the major cities. For example, you only need to walk through the streets of Lavapies in the centre of Madrid to hear different Arabic languages. This new diversity, together with the deteriorating economic situation, led the Spanish population to feel threatened.

As the spokesman for SOS Racismo (an NGO with French origins) mentioned in an interview with BBC Mundo.com in August 2011, racism is not particular to the right-wing but is also exhibited by people who are left-wing but "do not accept immigration as something ordinary and part of every day life". Indeed, long are the days of blatant political incorrectness when the chocolate-coated *Conguitos* were advertised by an African in "regional dress" or when pop singers unashamedly sang lyrics such as *"Todos los negritos tienen hambre y frío"* (all the black people are hungry and cold) but there is still a long way to go for the average Spaniard to view other nationalities and races beyond the stereotypes they hold in their heads.

This distrust of immigrants is increased by the fact that immigration is perceived to be larger than it really is. Whereas official figures showed the number of residents with permits to be 12%, most people taking part in a survey thought the number was 23%. The fact that this increase in immigration has been accompanied by a rise in illegal immigrants probably helps to distort the real figure and increase mistrust.

Madrid 2009

I was in the Puerta del Sol, wandering around enjoying the buzz of Madrid against the backdrop of a city in all its architectural glory. When suddenly, a wave of 15 (or so) young, black men came flooding past. I noticed behind me, someone trying to hide, seeking refuge behind me and my (tall) boyfriend. Then I understood what was going on. The police had arrived and raided the Puerta del Sol, giving chase to the *mantas* (blankets), those illegal immigrants from Africa who, dreaming of a better life, had ended up selling illegal DVDs laid out on blankets, in the centre of Madrid.

During the year 2006, in what was termed *"la crisis de los cayucos"* (the canoe crisis), 31,245 people from Africa arrived in the Canary Islands pursuing the dream of being given a better chance at life in Europe. Another 7,224 arrived in Andalucía. These men, women and sometimes even children, risked their lives to get to Spain in *cayucos* or *pateras* (fishing vessels), hoping to start a new life.

Around that time, it wasn't uncommon to see on TV images of people arriving onto the shores of the Canary Islands completely exhausted from their journeys and sometimes, even dead. On 6th October 2009, there were reports of 21 vessels arriving in the coast of Spain in only 24 hours.

I remember watching on television a *patera* full of African men arriving on the coast of one of the Canary Islands. The people who were calmly and pleasantly sunbathing on the beach did not run away. They did not begin to shout at them. Instead, they ran towards them with their towels to give them warmth and aid.

Unfortunately this kind of welcoming behaviour does not hit the headlines often and xenophobic attacks are as common in Spain as they are in any other countries where the population starts to diversify.

Xenophobic incidents continue to take place throughout the country. The Internet is full of newspaper articles and blog posts reporting xenophobic attacks on people from Ecuador, Senegal, Congo and Colombia as well as reports of chants in football stadiums, such as those experienced by the Brazilian football player Dani Alves. In 2006, there were over 4,000 attacks on immigrants and dozens of rather worrying racist demonstrations organized by neo-fascists and far-right groups. (As a comparison, that same year there were 56,000 similar attacks in the UK.)

We can only hope that, as the Spanish get through a long period of youth unemployment and economic instability, future generations will become blind to differences in race and will learn to love their neighbours, whatever the colour of their skin.

Changing Populations

By 2050, Spain will lose approximately 11 % of it population as the over 65's generation will form over 33% of the nation. Declining birth rates have highlighted a worrying future in which an ever diminishing working population will have to support an ever ageing majority.

During the first decade of the 21st century, Spain's working population was boosted by immigrants, but once the crisis hit and unemployment figures rocketed, many returned to their countries of origin whilst Spain's youth went abroad in search of work.

Perhaps one way of addressing the threat of a decrease in population was a new law introduced in 2015 inviting back to Spain up to 3.5 million Sephardic Jews. The law grants dual citizenship to those with Spanish ancestry in recognition of the wrong carried out when the Jewish community were exiled after the *Reconquista* in 1492.

It remains to be seen if the government will extend such an invitation to the Arabs and Moors that were similarly exiled.

Y is for Yo

How important is your name to define who you are? How important is it to those around you? How do you choose a name for a child?

In Spain, there are two days in the year when you get to celebrate who you are: your birthday and your saint's day, which is determined by your name. (*Yo*, by the way, means "I".)

Your saint's day would be the day dedicated to the saint with your same name, as decided by the Catholic Church. Usually, this will be on the day when the Saint died or when he or she performed a memorable act.

There are, however, exceptions to the rule. For example, my name is *Pilar*, so my saint's day is on 12th October. This is a public holiday in Spain, which also commemorates the day in which Columbus discovered America. *El día del Pilar* is the day in which the virgin Mary appeared on top of a pillar (*pilar*) to one of Christ's apostles in the city of Zaragoza. What's interesting about this particular festivity is that, whereas this event is believed to have happened on the 2nd January, the saint's day is on 12th October. It looks like a range of factors were involved in the decision of when to set the holiday, including the deadline by which the church housing the divine marble pillar was to be built. For reasons unknown to me all my life (in fact, I never knew there was a 10 month gap between the apparition and the official saint's day until I began researching this book; and neither did my mother who had a much more Catholic upbringing than I did) the official holiday was set by the Catholic Church as the 12th October.

The 12th October is not the only religious date set as a holiday thanks to its patron saint. The 19th March is San José and is a public holiday in many regions; 8th December is *El día de la Inmaculada* (say *"feliz santo"* to all those called Inma) and the 15th August is a celebration of the virgin's ascent to Heaven, so make sure you ring up all your friends called Asunción.

In addition to having a range of saint's days, the 1st November is also a public holiday: *el día de todos los santos* is dedicated to all those saints who weren't allocated their own date. It's also the date where those who want to pray for their dead loved ones can visit the church for a special mass blessing the souls of all those who passed away.

Another day dedicated to remembering others is the 28th December, *el día de los Santos Inocentes* (the day of the innocent saints). Although it is not a public holiday in itself, it does fall in the middle of the festive season. This day commemorates the massacre led by King Herod of all the innocent boys who were under two years of age after Christ was born. Strange then, that this day is commemorated by playing all kinds of jokes on each other, similar to those which take place on April Fool's day in the Anglo-Saxon world.

On 28th December, if you sit down with a family with children, be prepared to watch a plastic insect emerge from your lump of sugar as it dissolves, or to find a paper man stuck to your back or to be scared to death as your cigarette explodes as you light up. All these *inocentadas,* as well as those carried out in the media, form part of this tradition that has strangely emerged from a very sombre event.

Los puentes

You can see how saints have provided Spain with plenty of holidays. However, not content with the number of official holidays they have a year (about 12), a long time ago, the Spanish created a new form of day off: *el puente* (the bridge). The *puente* can turn odd days off into mini-holidays. For example, if 12th October falls on a Tuesday, there will be a holiday formed as you join the festive Sunday to the festive Tuesday via the Monday. Although not officially a day off everywhere, many people will not go to work (or school) on that day, being able to take a holiday from Saturday to Tuesday.

At one point, it looked like the *puente* might be coming to an end. In November 2011, the leader of the right-wing *Partido Popular* Mariano Rajoy was elected president. In December, he announced that one of the measures he was going to take to tackle the Spanish economic crisis was to move all public holidays to Mondays, to avoid the negative effects the *puentes* were having on the country's economy. Watch this space (or the Spanish news) to see whether the *puentes* are eventually demolished or not.

The saints and the holy family still influence how parents name their children. *Jesús* is not an uncommon name (it's also what you say to people when you hear them sneeze); many girls still have *María* as part of their name: María del Carmen, María del Mar. My mother had to fight with the priest in the 70s to be able to name me just *Pilar* instead of the much holier *María del Pilar*, which is the name on her I.D.

Identity

I can't help but comment on the fact that everyone in Spain carries an I.D. card with them - in fact, it's the law, you must carry it on you at all times. It is the best way of proving that you are who you are. It's also handy for when you pay with a credit card in person: you show your I.D. as you pay with your credit card (although I am not sure of whether this has had an effect on fraud prevention). The I.D. has your name on it, as well as your parents' first names.

It used to be very common to name children after their parents. I was named after my mother, my two cousins were named after *their* parents. This can become confusing if the son is named after the father as it will result in two people being called by the same name. However, you have to remember that in Spain, people take their father's surname as their first surname and their mother's surname as their second one. It is therefore unusual to find two people with exactly the same first name and combination of surnames. (Although sometimes people with the more common surnames end up with a double surname e.g. Francisco Martínez Martínez.)

This tradition of naming children after their parents is gradually disappearing as Spanish names are abandoned for more exotic sounding names from abroad.

Finally, I can't end a chapter dedicated to the letter "Y" without talking about the change in name that this letter itself has gone through in recent years. What used to be called the *i griega* (the Greek I) is now referred to as the "eye". Makes sense when the letter "i" was the only one to be named after its long lost cousin.

Z is for Zarzuela

Zarzuela has no translation, for it's an original form of art: Spain's very own style of musical theatre. I can't say it's very popular now, but it did enjoy periods of great splendour. The form began to take shape in the 16th and 17th centuries, at the same time as opera. Unlike opera however, straight dialogue is interspersed with musical numbers and there is no use of the recitative. As such, two of the most prolific playwrights, Lope de Vega and Calderón de la Barca, also wrote zarzuelas, with Calderón being the first to be credited with writing one of these works.

Although the *zarzuelas* were born during the Golden Age, their popularity soon declined and they became almost an endangered species until mid 18th century. Their name comes from the *Palacio de la Zarzuela* (Zarzuela Palace), where the Royal Family resides. The palace had been built by King Felipe IV to provide his brother with a place for recreation. When his brother left to rule Flandes, Felipe decided to put the palace to good use, making it available to musicians and artists. Actors were invited to entertain the Royals and their guests on those days when they couldn't go hunting and so, a new form of entertainment emerged: the *fiestas Zarzuela*.

The *zarzuelas* originally had mythical characters and stories at their centre. However, when the genre became popular in the 18th century, the stories began to be set in the "true Madrid", using ostentatious sets depicting the streets of the capital.

While the *zarzuela* hasn't evolved much in the last decades, the quality of dance continues to improve in the country. In 1979, Victor Ullate formed the National Ballet company and now runs a dance academy which has formed dancers of international reputation, such as Tamara Rojo, who used to be principal dancer in the UK's Royal National Ballet and then became Artistic Director of the English National Ballet.

In addition to the Madrid-centred genre, *zarzuela* is also used to describe a dish originating in Barcelona. The *zarzuela de pescados y mariscos* (fish and shellfish zarzuela) is a stew full of seasonal fish and seafood, sometimes accompanied with a sauce containing nuts.

But before I go off on another food tangent, let me come back to the performing arts in Spain.

The *zarzuela* is still alive and kicking in Spain but its popularity has definitely waned. That does not mean that the musical genre is not popular in Spain. *"Al contrario"*.

Spanish Broadway

In 1992, the West End musical arrived in Spain. There had been some Spanish versions of musicals produced before ('Jesus Christ Superstar' and 'Evita', for example) but 'Les Miserables' definitely marked the start of the musical in the cultural centres of Spain.

The libretto of 'Les Mis' was translated by José Tamayo, who had set up the *Teatro de Bellas Artes* in Madrid and was responsible for exporting a range of *zarzuelas* (of the musical kind, not the fish). Tamayo also produced the show along with Plácido

Domingo, the great opera singer, conductor and general great cultural ambassador for Spain. Though I was a bit sceptical about a Spanish version of 'Les Mis', I managed to grab some tickets when it first opened. The acting was fantastic and even though some of the translations just couldn't match the English (*Rojo* having two syllables doesn't quite have the same punch as "red"), *'Los miserables'* hooked the Spanish public and paved the way for other West End and Broadway shows such as 'The Lion King', 'Chicago' and 'Mamma Mia'.

Inspired by this last show, Nacho Cano (from the successful pop group Mecano) and others produced *'Hoy no me puedo levantar'* ('I can't get up today'). The title was the first line of Mecano's 80s hit *'Maquillaje'* ('Make-up') and therefore, it spoke volumes to the Spanish public. The musical was full of songs by Mecano and reflected life in the 80s during *la movida*. The show opened in 2005 and closed in 2011, after which a spin-off cast created 'M.K.2.0', the story of Mecano.

So, Spanish theatre definitely has its commercial side. The musicals, the classics (which still pack them in) and the comedies featuring actors who've made it on T.V.

Luckily theatre did diversify during the end of last century, with the growth of small studio theatres which are now part of the programme of festivals like the *Festival de Otoño en Primavera* (Autumn Festival in Spring). Yes, you read right. In 2010, the subsidised *Festival de Otoño* in Madrid was moved from the dark Autumn season which was saturated with programming from the private theatres, to the brighter, warmer Spring. The festival had already built a reputation with audiences and artists alike;

some of the programming included internationally respected artists and companies such as Peter Brook, Uta Lemper and Robert Lepage. Not wanting to throw away the reputation and following the *Festival de Otoño* had built, but realising that it could attract larger audience members at a different time of year, the then president of the Comunidad de Madrid Esperanza Aguirre moved the festival to a different place in the calendar and spun its original name.

Spanish Theatre

Els Joglars is an ensemble-based company which has been experimenting with theatre styles while unashamedly making political and social comments since 1962. Initially led by Albert Boadella, the company is still one of the most irreverent yet successful Spanish theatre companies to have achieved international success.

Els Joglars' 'Daaalí', which I saw in both Madrid and London, transported audiences into the mind of the surrealist painter Dalí as he lay moribund in his hospital bed. This was one of the most beautiful pieces of theatre I have ever seen, elevating Els Joglars' style to a different plane while still maintaining their characteristic humour and bite. Els Joglars celebrated their 50th anniversary in 2011, surviving the departure of Albert Boadella, who ran the Teatros del Canal in Madrid from 2008 - 2016.

An even bolder, more subversive collective of artists is La Fura dels Baus who not only play with form as they try to shock the audience, but they also play with space. La Fura, who have their origins in street theatre, have created spectacles as diverse as the opening of the Barcelona 1992 Olympics, the opera 'La Grande Macabre' and the controversial 'XXX', which made it to the front page of London's Evening Standard tabloid when it toured to the Riverside Studios. The piece, based on the work by Marat Sade, was indeed X-rated and attracted a small "let's stop this show" demonstration on its opening night. This left the company members baffled, especially considering that a certain British tabloid famously features topless ladies on its page 3.

Not happy with shocking the audience and playing with their emotions, La Fura also built their own space in the sea: a boat able to host a series of performances to tour around the world, which goes by the name of 'Naumon'.

Madrid and Cataluña have traditionally always been at "war". Although I was born and bred in Madrid, I never felt a strong antagonism towards the Catalans. The fact that I hold both Els Joglars and La Fura dels Baus dear to my heart (the former for inspiring me during my teenage years and the latter because I did a short stint of work for them in London) proves that people are people and enjoying life together is possible no matter where you're from.

Spanish Cinema

Although not recognised worldwide for excelling in the performing arts, the Spanish continue to innovate and evolve. Leading the way in the commercial world is Pedro Almodóvar, Oscar-winner and mentor of many actors, who helped launch the international careers of Antonio Banderas and Penélope Cruz. Following his popularity steps, albeit at a purely national level, is Santiago Segura. In 1998, he created what has become a powerful franchise and produced his first hit film: *'Torrente: el brazo tonto de la ley'* ("Torrente: the Stupid Arm of the Law"). Torrente is a filthy, disgusting cop, an antihero. The Spanish love their spoofs (see **E is for Euro**) and this series of films featuring policeman Torrente have become an absolute phenomenon in Spain. His last offering seemed to aim to attract the international market as it was released under the English title: 'Torrente 4. Lethal Crisis'.

Coda

So, that's it. That was *The A to Z of Spanish Culture* as told by Pilar Orti. Writing the book was great fun. I found out the origins of traditions I'd grown up with but had never questioned; I relived episodes from my childhood and my youth; I found out the things I liked and disliked about Spain and realised how strong an opinion I hold about the country and her people.

Distance has given me... distance, the ability to look at aspects of my life from afar, but it has also brought me closer to a culture that, though part of me, I have voluntarily left behind.

Before I say good-bye, allow me to leave you with those who still live in Spain who have helped me to bring my own knowledge up to date. '***From the Horses' Mouths***' includes the notes that my friends and family have sent me, in their original Spanish and with English translations.

Do get in touch if you enjoyed the book or if you have found any outrageous errors in it. My personal blog is www.pilarwrites.com and my Twitter handle is @PilarOrti, although I mainly tweet about the future of work and virtual teams. (And if that sounds interesting to you, check out www.virtualnotdistant.com)

If you want to find out more about what's going on in Spain, checkout my podcast Spain Uncovered. I'm not releasing any new episodes, but there are plenty of them out there to keep you entertained for a while. (And if you've enjoyed my personal stories, there are lots more in my memoir *Hi, I'm Here for a*

Recording. The ordinary life of a voiceover artist.) And if you have a minute, do leave a review for the book on the platform you purchased it from. It might well help someone else decide whether they want to read it or not.

Finally, I hope the book was useful, or of interest or that, at least, at some point, it made you think differently or just smile.

Acknowledgements

Thanks to:

Paul Read for helping me bring the book up to date. I wouldn't have done it on my own.

My mother for her constant, active support and help with this project (and with all my projects).

My father for suggesting *Amor* as a better alternative to *Abarrotado*; and Ivor for helping me to flesh it out.

Tomás en Europa for showing me through his blog that it is o.k. to speak your mind in a public space.

Estefania for making sure I got it right and showing she liked it by passing the first draft on to her sister.

My cousins Pachi, Sonia and Tomás for their help, support and contributions.

Simon for always getting the balance between being critical and encouraging just right.

Meri for her continuous readership and comments on the blog.

Dan for helping me create a chapter out of a W.C. idea.

Manuel for his contribution to the Spanglish Project and for this cover.

Thanks to Simon for the formatting.

Thanks to Sam, Neil and Rowan at Alchemy Post in London for the audiobook recording.

The Writers and Bloggers in Spain Facebook group, what a bunch of talented entrepreneurs! As long as there are guys like you in Spain, the country has a future.

And last but first: thanks to Kevin, the Pin to my Pon.

Vocabulary

Introduction

"Pero eso... va a ser mucho trabajo."

(But that is going to be a lot of work.)

Guay. Similar to "cool".

A is for Amor

Cafeterías. A mixture between a café and a bar.

Pandillas. Gangs, usually of teenagers.

Atasco. Traffic jam.

En caravana. Traffic in caravan style, cars almost directly in front of each other, travelling at the same speed.

En cadena. One after the other (chain reaction).

Operación salida and *operación retorno.* Terms used at the beginning and end of the holiday season.

Alta Velocidad Española. High Speed Spanish train (AVE).

Valencianos. Those from Valencia.

Cava. Spanish sparkling wine.

Camareros, camareras. Waiters and waitresses.

Rimas. Rhymes.

Los suspiros son aire y van al aire.

Las lágrimas son agua y van al mar.

Dime, mujer, cuando el amor se olvida

¿sabes tú adónde va?

Sighs are made of air and so return to the air.

Tears are made of water and so return to the sea.

Tell me, woman, when love is forgotten,

Where does it return to?

B is for Botellón

Botellón. The modern term given to the gathering of young people in an open space, drinking alcohol mainly by sharing bottles.

Botella. Bottle.

Litrona. A bottle of 1 litre, usually of beer/lager.

Mini, cachis. A drink of one litre.

Leche de pantera. Panther's milk: a cocktail made of rum, milk and cinnamon.

Caña. A small measure of beer/lager.

Aperitivo. Aperitif.

Copas. Alcoholic drinks, mixers. Also the physical wine glass.

Vino con gaseosa. Wine with soda.

Carajillo. Coffee with brandy.

Chupitos. Shots of spirits.

Pacharán. An anisette-based alcoholic drink.

Controles de alcoholemia. Alcohol beverage police controls.

Si bebes, no conduzcas. If you drink, don't drive.

Portero or *conserje.* The concierge.

Quiosco. A free-standing newsagents.

Chucherías. Sweets and other deliciously addictive foods like *chicles* (chewing gum) and *gusanitos* (corn puffs).

Estancos. Shops where you can buy tobacco and other things.

Mercería. Haberdashery.

Ferretería. Shop with everything you'll need for the home: screws, tools, taps…

Una barra de pan. A stick of French bread.

Panadería. Bakery.

Cuernos, huge pastries covered in chocolate with liquid chocolate inside.

Cartera. Schoolbag.

"¡Ahí va!" Common Spanish exclamation, usually following a realisation.

Pastelitos. Small *pasteles,* or cakes.

Frutería, verdulería, carnicería, pescadería. Fruit store, grocery store, butchers, fishmonger's.

Mercado. Market.

Mancomunidad. Managing agent.

Reuniones de vecinos. Residents' meetings or literally, meetings of neighbours.

C is for Corona

La corona. The crown; the monarchy.

"¿Qué pasa?" "What's going on?"

Guardia civil. The civil guard, the military police.

Tricornio. Three-pointed hat worn by the civil guards.

"Quieto todo el mundo." "Everyone, stand still."

"Al suelo, al suelo todo el mundo." "Everyone, down on the floor."

"No intentes apuntar la cámara que te mato." "Don't try to point the camera or I'll kill you."

La Transición. The transition from dictatorship to democracy after Franco.

"¿Por qué no te callas?" "Why don't you shut up?"

Efecto mariposa: yo pago mis impuestos en España y un elefante muere en Botsuana. The Butterfly Effect: I pay my taxes in Spain and an elephant dies in Botswana.

D is for Duende

Duende, a small, elf-like, magical creature; a concept of divine, artistic inspiration, which gives the performer an edge, a unique spine-chilling effect.

El espíritu oculto de la dolorida España. The hidden spirit of the Spain in pain.

El duende no está en la garganta; el duende sube por dentro desde la planta de los pies. Duende is not in the throat; duende surges through your insides from the soles of your feet.

"Tú tienes voz, tú sabes de estilos, pero no triunfarás nunca

porque tú no tienes duende." "You have a voice, you know about styles, but you'll never make it because you don't have duende."

Guiri. Foreigner (slang).

Qué dirán. What will people say?

E is for Euro

Pesetas. Old Spanish currency.

Mil eurista. Young person who survives on 1,000 Euros a month.

Todo bajo el sol. Everything under the sun.

F is for Fútbol

Héroe nacional. National hero.

La roja. The red one.

Siempre con nosotros. Always with us, will always will be with us.

G is for Goya

Fusilamientos de tres de mayo. The third of May executions.

Los desastres de la guerra. The war disasters.

Pinturas negras. Black paintings.

Saturno devorando a su hijo. Saturn devouring his son.

La quinta del sordo. The deaf man's home.

Las hilanderas. The women who spin.

Meninas. Maids of honour.

Aposentador. Chamberlain.

H is for Hola

Hijo. Son.

Hola. Hello.

Buenos días. Good morning.

Buenas tardes. Good afternoon.

¿Qué tal? How are you?

Encantado/a. Glad to (meet you).

¿Dígame? Lit. Tell me, used when answering the phone.

I is for Inglés

Inglés. English.

"*Me voy a Londres.*" "I'm going to London."

"*¿A qué?*" "What for?"

"*A aprender inglés.*" "To learn English."

Los ingleses. The English.

Gallegos. Galicians.

J is for Joder

Joder. Fuck.

"*¡Joder con los plastas estos!*" Damn these annoying people!

Pesados. Lit. Heavy; annoying.

¡Deja ya de joder! Stop bugging me!

Yo no me llamo Javier. My name is not Javier.

Toreros muertos. Dead bullfighters.

Gilipollas. Idiot.

Chiste. Joke.

Cagarla. To mess it up. (Lit. To poo.)

Marrón. Brown. Can also mean a messy situation.

Pasar. To pass.

K is for Kilómetro

Kilómetro. Kilometre.

Cuarto y mitad. A quarter and a half.

Carreteras radiales. Radius roads.

L is for Laico

Estado laico. Secular state.

Declaración de hacienda. Tax return.

Primera comunión. First communion.

M is for Movida

Movida. 80s movement. Lit. "Moved"

Destape. Uncovering.

Bola de cristal. Crystal ball.

Rombos. Rhombuses.

Indignados. Indignant. (2010's movement.)

N is for Nupcias

Nupcias. Marriage.

Segundas nupcias. Second marriage.

Boda. Wedding.

Casarse. Get married.

Novios. Boyfriend and girlfriend or bride and groom.

¡Vivan los novios! Long live the bride and groom!

Hermana. Sister.

Madre. Mother.

¡Que se besen! Come on, kiss!

Beso. Kiss.

Lista de bodas. Wedding list.

Barra libre. Free bar.

Ñ is for Ñ

Maño. From Zaragoza.

Año. Year.

Ano. Anus.

Español/a. Spaniard.

Sabio. Wise.

Castellano. Castilian.

Gallego. Galician.

Catalán. Catalan.

Vasco. Basque.

Comunidades autónomas. Autonomous regions.

Facha. Fascist.

O is for ¡Olé!

Pase. Bullfighter's cape movement as the bull passes him/her. Anything that has to do with passing, also passing the ball in football, for example.

Sin problema. No problem.

La casa. The house.

El cielo. The sky.

La fiesta nacional. Lit. The national feast. Refers to bullfighting.

Encierro. Bulls running after you.

Gigantes. Giants.

Cabezudos. Big-heads.

Moros. Moors.

Cristianos. Christians.

Trilogía. Trilogy.

Olleta alcoyana. Casserole-type dish from Alcoy (Alicante).

Morcilla. Sausage, black-pudding like.

Procesiones. Processions.

Horchata. Drink made from tigernut.

Fartón. Pastry made from wheat.

P is for Paraguas

Paraguas. Umbrella.

Aguas. Waters.

Para. Stop or "for".

Q is for Quijote

Quijote. A man who resembles the main character of Cervantes' novel by the same name.

"En un lugar de la mancha, de cuyo nombre no quiero acordarme…"

In a place in La Mancha, the name of which I don't wish to remember…

Quijotada. An action typical of the Quijote.

Entremeses. Snacks or food served before the meals. One-act plays.

Oveja. Sheep.

Comendador. Military commander.

Venganza. Revenge.

Matanza. Massacre.

Delicado. Delicate.

R is for Refrán

Refrán. Proverb.

Dichos. Sayings.

Andarse por las ramas. Beating around the bush.

Más vale pájaro en mano, que ciento volando. Better to have a bird in your hand, than 100 flying.

De perdidos al río. From lost to the river.

A quien madruga, Dios le ayuda. God helps whoever gets up early.

En casa del herrero, cuchillo de palo. In the ironmonger's house, use a wooden knife.

De tal palo, tal astilla. From such a stick, you get such a splinter.

Perro ladrador, poco mordedor. Barking dog bites little.

Del dicho al hecho, hay un buen trecho. From saying to doing, there's a good distance.

Tirar la casa por la ventana. Throwing the house out of the window.

Te he dicho mil veces... I've told you a thousand times...

S is for Sobremesa y Siesta

Sobremesa. The period of time after lunch.

Chupito. Small amount of liqueur, usually served after a meal.

Bocadillo. Sandwhich made of French bread. (Slang: *bocata*.)

Plato combinado. Mixed dish.

Menú del día. Daily menu.

Culebrón. Soap opera.

Culebra. Snake.

Sangría. Drink made mainly with red wine and lemonade.

T is for Tapas

Tapas. Small portions of food served mainly with drink. *Tapar* means to cover.

Salchichón. Type of salami.

Aceitunas. Olives.

Patatas. Potatoes, crisps.

Corteza. Pork scratchings.

Primer plato. Starter. Lit. First dish.

Segundo plato. Main course. Lit. Second dish.

Ración. Portion.

Patatas bravas. "Brave potatoes".

Huevos. Eggs.

Estrellados. Smashed.

Rotos. Broken.

Jamón. Ham.

Melón. Melon.

Chorizo. Spicy sausage.

Calamar. Squid.

Tortilla. Omelette.

Ajo. Garlic.

Pollo. Chicken.

Arroz. Rice.

U is for Uvas

Uvas. Grapes.

Peladas. Peeled, from the verb *pelar*, to peel.

Pites. Stones (from the grapes).

Campanadas. Bell chimes.

Suerte. Luck.

Primera. First.

Martes y trece. Tuesday 13th.

Cuartos. Quarters.

Zambomba. A rustic instrument typical of Christmas time.

Belén. Bethlehem. Also refers to the collection of miniatures depicting the Birth of Christ in Bethlehem.

Los tres reyes magos. The three wise men.

Cabalgatas. Parades.

Noche de reyes. Twelfth Night. Lit. Night of the Kings.

Carbón. Coal, which can be *dulce*, sweet.

Roscón. Ring-like cake eaten on 6th January.

Relleno. Filling.

Nata. Cream.

V is for Vino

Vino. Wine.

Gaseosa. Soda.

Calimocho. Wine with Coke.

Tinto. Red wine.

Bodega. Cellar.

W is for W.C.

Bonus phrase: ¿Dónde están los baños? Where are the toilets?

Retrete. Toilet.

Inodoro. Posh way of saying toilet.

X is for Xenofobia

España es simpatía. Sea amable con los turistas. Es fácil porque somos así.

Spain is friendliness. Be kind to tourists. It's easy because we are made that way.

Manta. Blanket.

Cayuco. Canoe.

Patera. Canoe.

Y is for Yo

Yo. Me.

Feliz santo. Happy Saint's Day.

El día de todos los santos. All Saint's Day.

Inocente. Innocent.

Puente. Bridge.

Z is for Zarzuela

Zarzuela. Spanish style of musical theatre.

Palacio. Palace.

Pescado. Fish.

Marisco. Shellfish.

Hoy no me puedo levantar. I can't get up today.

Otoño. Autumn.

Primavera. Spring.

Brazo. Arm.

Tonto. Stupid.

Ley. Law.

From The Horses' Mouths

One of the most interesting things about writing this book has been hearing about customs and traditions which I might not have experienced directly. Here are some examples of what some of my friends have commented in reply to my chapters or questions.

I am also including here a list of links to articles that have been used to update the third edition.

B is for Botellón

Sonia said:

Para el botellón voy a tener q explicarte las formas de botellón q no salían en la tele y q hacíamos los universitarios, según pachi eran botellones pijos, en parques de zonas de oficina, con vasos de tubo de plástico, bolsas de hielo para preparar las copas individuales y patatas para picar. Había zonas como metropolitano donde existían locales en los q únicamente vendían packs de vasos de tubo, la botella de alcohol, hielo, refresco de dos litros y aperitivos. Los minis estaban descartados, bebíamos copas y éramos todos universitarios, y al terminar recogíamos, el horario era de diez a como muchísimo las dos, y a esa hora nos íbamos a bares. No todo el botellón era ruido y suciedad. Tengo a reivindicar mis viejas costumbres de juventud.

Regarding the Botellón, I'm going to have to tell you about the types of botellón they never showed on T.V and that we, the university students, took part in; according to Pachi they were posh botellones, in the parks of office grounds, with plastic tube glasses, bags of ice to prepare individual drinks and crisps to snack on. There were some areas like Metropolitano, where there were shops where they only sold "packs" with tube glasses, a bottle of alcohol, ice, two litre bottles of soft drinks and snacks. The minis were rejected, we drank "copas" (drink prepared in a glass) and we were all at university. When we'd finish we cleared up after ourselves; we'd drink from ten o'clock to about two at the latest and then we'd go into the bars. Not every botellón was noisy and dirty. I have to claim back the traditions from my youth.

C is for Corona

https://politica.elpais.com/politica/2017/02/17/actuali-dad/1487318715_211475.html

http://www.theguardian.com/world/2014/jun/25/spain-princess-cristina-court-corruption-urdangarin

http://www.theguardian.com/world/2016/jan/10/king-of-spain-sister-infanta-cristina-court-tax-evasion-charges

http://www.theguardian.com/world/2014/jun/05/princess-aunt-stirs-up-republican-support-against-monarchy-in-spain

https://twitter.com/HenarOrtiz/status/473772853356019712

G is for Goya

Regarding El Greco.
My mother said:
Quizás podrías decir que Creta era un protectorado Veneciano y que por eso él se fué allí a pintar donde conoció a Tiziano, Tintoretto y Verones que influenciaron en cierto modo su pintura (de Tiziano el volumen y movimiento de los cuerpos por ejemplo).

Era un extraordinario retratista, y pinta a muchos coetáneos suyos, concentrando todo su interés en la faz y las manos, con una tecnica de grandes y sueltas pinceladas ocres y grises, como haría despues Frans Hals, de la escuela holandesa. En muchos de sus cuadros aparece Toledo, como paisaje de fondo.

Tiene cuadros diseminados por las galerías de todo el mundo, (aparte de las españolas e iglesias y conventos), tales como washington, New York, Minneapolis Philadelfia, Copenhagen, Budapest, etc.

Se dice que hacía modelos de cera que copiaba despuñes en sus telas, que efectivamente tienen la misma calidad y flexibilidad de la cera y su misma calidad irreal. (No sé si puedes ver su San Sebastián para que te hagas una idea.) Usa los tonos puros, recortados por gruesas líneas negras y para dar volumen a las ropas utiliza empastes gruesos de pintura (o sea capa encima de capa, todas las que necesite). Se dice que su pincelada es de un gran valor expresivo, al ser tan suelta, como inacabada, como el inundar de lágrimas un ojo sólo con una pincelada blanca, dada verticalmente sobre la pupila.

Maybe you could say that Crete was under the protection of Venice and that is why he went to there to paint and met Tiziano, Tintoretto and Verones who influenced his style of painting (from Tiziano, for example, he learnt about the volume and movement of bodies.)

He was an extraordinary portrait artist and painted many people of his age, concentrating all his interest on the face and hands, with a technique which uses large and loose brushstrokes using ochre and grey colours, just as the Dutch Frans Hals would later do. Toledo appears in many of his paintings as a backdrop.

He has paintings dispersed in galleries all over the world (in addition to the Spanish ones, churches and convents) such as Washington, New York, Minneapolis, Philadelphia, Copenhagen, Budapest, etc.

They say he made wax models first which he then copied into canvas, which indeed have the same quality and flexibility as wax and have the same unrealistic quality. (Not sure whether you can have a look at his San Sebastian, to see what I mean.) He uses pure tones, cut by thick

*black lines. To give volume to the clothes, he uses thick
paint fillings (that is, layer upon layer, however many he
needs). His brushstroke has great expressive value, as it is
loose, almost unfinished, like when he floods an eye with
tears with just one white brushstroke, vertically placed
over the pupil.*

M is also for Menuda Movida

http://www.theguardian.com/world/2016/sep/02/third-spanish-
election-likely-after-attempt-to-form-government-fails

http://www.theguardian.com/world/2015/may/25/
spains-indignados-ada-colau-elections-mayor-barcelona

http://www.theguardian.com/world/datablog/2015/dec/21/
spanish-elections-unprecedented-result-what-happens-next

http://www.theguardian.com/world/2016/jun/12/
unidos-podemos-spain-election-leftwing-alliance-united-left

http://www.huffingtonpost.es/2017/11/16/correa-afronta-la-pe-
ticion-de-125-anos-de-carcel-en-el-final-del-juicio-de-la-prim-
era-etapa-del-caso-gurtel_a_23280087/

http://www.theguardian.com/world/2016/oct/04/
spanish-politicians-court-corruption-case-trial-year

http://www.theguardian.com/world/2009/mar/06/
spain-opposition-corruption-scandal

http://www.theguardian.com/world/2017/jul/26/mariano-rajoy-
becomes-first-serving-spanish-pm-to-testify-in-criminal-case

http://www.elmundo.es/elmundo/2013/07/14/
espana/1373779073.html

O is for ¡Olé!

Regarding the *sevillanas*.
Tomasito said:
Es cierto que hay mucha cultura popular alrededor de ellas (las sevillanas), y que a veces se desvían un poco de lo que parece más flamenco "serio", por llamarlo de alguna forma. Pero las Sevillanas son un palo del flamenco con su estructura rítmica y armónica propia, si se plantea desde un punto de vista musical. Aunque a lo mejor tampoco es necesario tanto tecnicismo.

It's true that there is a lot of popular culture around the sevillanas and that sometimes they deviate from the more "serious" flamenco, to call it something. But the sevillanas are a branch of flamenco with their own rhythmic and harmonic structure if you are looking at it from a musical point of view. Although maybe we don't need all these technicalities.

O is for ¡Olé!

Regarding the *fallas*.

Pachi said:

Fiestas tradicionales valencianas, que han sabido conservar el espíritu popular, hasta donde lo permiten los tiempos modernos. Antiguamente, se financiaban íntegramente con aportaciones de los vecinos y empresarios de los barrios donde se levantaba el monumento. Hoy día, por su interés "cultural", la financiación mayoritaria corre a cargo de organismos públicos (ayuntamiento, distritos, etc.).

El reinado de la pólvora, organizada (despertá, nit del foc, cordás y mascletás), y desorganizada (la guerra en la calle). Las despertás se hacen a las 8 de la mañana, quemando pólvora para avisar a los vecinos que empieza la jornada; las mascletás empiezan el primer domingo de marzo; los castillos de fuego se concentran los sábados, hasta el último fin de semana, que se queman uno al día –el del día 18 es el castillo estrella-; y las cordás, muy restringidas y controladas, por accidentes pasados –no me extraña-.

Las tardes de los días de fallas: o se participa o visita el engalanamiento floral de la Virgen de los Desamparados (la cheperudeta, es decir, la jorobadita, en valenciano), o se va a dormir la siesta, porque el resto del día y noche estarán ocupados. Los amantes de los toros tienen las primeras corridas grandes de la temporada taurina, que se abre en la plaza de Toros de Valencia, corridas de San José.

Traditional festivities in Valencia, which have been able to preserve the popular spirit, up to where modern times have allowed them to. In past times, they were financed completely by the neighbours' contributions and by the local businessmen. Today, due to their "cultural interest", most of the funding comes from public bodies (Mayor, districts etc.)

The reign of gunpowder: both organised (despertá, nit del foc, cordás *and* mascletás) *and not organised (the war in the street). The* despertás *happen at 8 in the morning, lighting up gunpowder to alert the population that the day has begun; the* mascletás *begin on the first Sunday in March; the castles of fire gather on Saturdays, until the last weekend, when they are burnt one a day: the one burnt on the 18th is the star castle; and the* cordás*, restricted and controlled, due to past accidents - I'm not surprised.*

The afternoons of the fallas: you are either involved in or visiting the adornment of the Virgen de los Desamparados *(the* cheperudeta*, that is, the hunchback in Valenciá) or they go to have a siesta, because for the rest of the day and night, they are busy. Those who love bullfighting can watch the first big bullfights of the season, which starts in the Plaza de Toros de Valencia, with the* corridas de San José.

T is for Tapas

I asked on various social networks what the English for the *fideo* found in *fideúa* was called in English. Here is what *Martin said:*

Well, if not vermicelli, then two other possible types. If its the long thin ones (often cut up) it could be capellini. These are finer than vermicelli. Sometimes go by the name of angel hair in English. Or, if it's the little short pasta, like half a bicycle tyre, sort of a letter C, with a hole through the middle, then probably chifferini. (I only know that cos I saw them in a Portuguese deli yesterday!)

About the Authors

Pilar Orti

Pilar lived in Madrid until the age of 18. Her upbringing was already a little bit unusual: at home, she was brought up by parents who had spent their adult formative years in Stanford, California. At school, her first written language was English, as were her teachers, if not her peers. Following the English education system at King's College in Madrid made her fall in love with the English language and way of studying. She also fell in love with theatre at an early age: she wrote, directed and acted in her first play when she was 7, ran her first theatre workshop when she was 10 and formed an amateur theatre company when she was 15.

Not having ever considered a career in the theatre, at 18, she left Spain to go to London to study Biology at Imperial College. Once there she realised she'd much rather read Peter Brook and Shakespeare than spend her time in the laboratory surrounded by petri dishes. The time had come to train as an actress, which she did, at Mountview Theatre School and then went on to set up Forbidden Theatre Company with a friend. Around that time (1997), she also discovered the world of Voiceover and realised she could earn a living by speaking into a microphone in Spanish. You can hear her voice in Spain if you watch some adverts or play with certain toys or video-games or if you watch the animation series GoJetters.

As technology has advanced and people no longer see the office as the main place where work and collaboration happens,

Pilar has set up Virtual not Distant® to help managers and leaders of virtual teams and those working from home. She's having fun having conversations about the world of work through the podcast "21st Century Work Life", available on all podcast platforms and applications. (www.virtualnotdistant.com)

Having parked aside her theatrical work, writing books, novels and poems allows Pilar to continue letting her imagination and language run free. If you have enjoyed the autobiographical nature of this book, check out "Hi, I'm Here for a Recording. The ordinary life of a voiceover artist." If you want to learn more about contemporary Spain, check out the Spain Uncovered podcast.

And if you want to practice your Spanish, listen to "En clave de podcast", a bilingual show about podcasting in Spain in 2016/2017.

Other Books by Pilar

Online Meetings that Rock *(in preparation)*
Hi, I'm Here for a Recording. The ordinary
life of a voiceover artist.
Your Handy Companion to Devising and Physical Theatre
When Five Years Pass, a translation of the
play by Federico García Lorca
Thriving Through Change at Work
Visibility in Virtual Teams
The Doodles, a children's story

Pilar on the Web

www.virtualnotdistant.com
www.pilarwrites.com

Paul Read

Paul Read travels back and forth between Devon in the UK and Andalucia, Spain, running workshops and recording material for his online Tai Chi school. In a parallel life, he continues to write about the history of Spain - having majored in Spanish Studies at the University of London. He continues to work on his 'Forgotten Stories from Spain' trilogy that looks at the significant role of individuals during the outset of the Spanish Civil War: the Canadian Doctor Norman Bethune, the English novelist George Orwell and the charismatic anarchist leader, Buenaventura Durruti.

Other Books by Paul

Forgotten Stories From Spain: The Ambulance Man And The Spanish Civil War
Forgotten Stories From Spain: 1984 And The Spanish Civil War
The Slow Route Home (The Radical Routes Series Book 1) Kindle Edition
Inside the Tortilla: A Journey in Search of Authenticity (The Radical Routes Series Book 2)

Paul on the Web

www.facebook.com/storiesfromspain
www.Speakingofspain.com

Made in the USA
Monee, IL
02 December 2019